"After utilizing toolkits [illegible] threats within my organiza[illegible] unaware. Using my team's knowledge as a competitive advantage, we now have superior systems that save time and energy."

"As a new Chief Technology Officer, I was feeling unprepared and inadequate to be successful in my role. I ordered an IT toolkit Sunday night and was prepared Monday morning to shed light on areas of improvement within my organization. I no longer felt overwhelmed and intimidated, I was excited to share what I had learned."

"I used the questionnaires to interview members of my team. I never knew how many insights we could produce collectively with our internal knowledge."

"I usually work until at least 8pm on weeknights. The Art of Service questionnaire saved me so much time and worry that Thursday night I attended my son's soccer game without sacrificing my professional obligations."

"After purchasing The Art of Service toolkit, I was able to identify areas where my company was not in compliance that could have put my job at risk. I looked like a hero when I proactively educated my team on the risks and presented a solid solution."

"I spent months shopping for an external consultant before realizing that The Art of Service would allow my team to consult themselves! Not only did we save time not catching a consultant up to speed, we were able to keep our company information and industry secrets confidential."

"Everyday there are new regulations and processes in my industry. The Art of Service toolkit has kept me ahead by using AI technology to constantly update the toolkits and address emerging needs."

"I customized The Art of Service toolkit to focus specifically on the concerns of my role and industry. I didn't have to waste time with a generic self-help book that wasn't tailored to my exact situation."

"Many of our competitors have asked us about our secret sauce. When I tell them it's the knowledge we have in-house, they never believe me. Little do they know The Art of Service toolkits are working behind the scenes."

"One of my friends hired a consultant who used the knowledge gained working with his company to advise their competitor. Talk about a competitive disadvantage! The Art of Service allowed us to keep our knowledge from walking out the door along with a huge portion of our budget in consulting fees."

"Honestly, I didn't know what I didn't know. Before purchasing The Art of Service, I didn't realize how many areas of my business needed to be refreshed and improved. I am so relieved The Art of Service was there to highlight our blind spots."

"Before The Art of Service, I waited eagerly for consulting company reports to come out each month. These reports kept us up to speed but provided little value because they put our competitors on the same playing field. With The Art of Service, we have uncovered unique insights to drive our business forward."

"Instead of investing extensive resources into an external consultant, we can spend more of our budget towards pursuing our company goals and objectives...while also spending a little more on corporate holiday parties."

"The risk of our competitors getting ahead has been mitigated because The Art of Service has provided us with a 360-degree view of threats within our organization before they even arise."

Salesforce CPQ
Complete Self-Assessment Guide

https://theartofservice.com
support@theartofservice.com

Table of Contents

About The Art of Service 9

Included Resources - how to access 9
Purpose of this Self-Assessment 11
How to use the Self-Assessment 12
Salesforce CPQ
Scorecard Example 14
Salesforce CPQ
Scorecard 15

BEGINNING OF THE
SELF-ASSESSMENT: 16
CRITERION #1: RECOGNIZE 17

CRITERION #2: DEFINE: 25

CRITERION #3: MEASURE: 39

CRITERION #4: ANALYZE: 50

CRITERION #5: IMPROVE: 65

CRITERION #6: CONTROL: 81

CRITERION #7: SUSTAIN: 92
Salesforce CPQ and Managing Projects, Criteria for Project
Managers: 135
1.0 Initiating Process Group: Salesforce CPQ 136

1.1 Project Charter: Salesforce CPQ 138

1.2 Stakeholder Register: Salesforce CPQ 140

1.3 Stakeholder Analysis Matrix: Salesforce CPQ 141

2.0 Planning Process Group: Salesforce CPQ 143

2.1 Project Management Plan: Salesforce CPQ 145
2.2 Scope Management Plan: Salesforce CPQ 147
2.3 Requirements Management Plan: Salesforce CPQ 149
2.4 Requirements Documentation: Salesforce CPQ 151
2.5 Requirements Traceability Matrix: Salesforce CPQ 153
2.6 Project Scope Statement: Salesforce CPQ 155
2.7 Assumption and Constraint Log: Salesforce CPQ 157
2.8 Work Breakdown Structure: Salesforce CPQ 159
2.9 WBS Dictionary: Salesforce CPQ 161
2.10 Schedule Management Plan: Salesforce CPQ 164
2.11 Activity List: Salesforce CPQ 166
2.12 Activity Attributes: Salesforce CPQ 168
2.13 Milestone List: Salesforce CPQ 170
2.14 Network Diagram: Salesforce CPQ 172
2.15 Activity Resource Requirements: Salesforce CPQ 174
2.16 Resource Breakdown Structure: Salesforce CPQ 176
2.17 Activity Duration Estimates: Salesforce CPQ 178
2.18 Duration Estimating Worksheet: Salesforce CPQ 180
2.19 Project Schedule: Salesforce CPQ 182

2.20 Cost Management Plan: Salesforce CPQ 184

2.21 Activity Cost Estimates: Salesforce CPQ 186

2.22 Cost Estimating Worksheet: Salesforce CPQ 188

2.23 Cost Baseline: Salesforce CPQ 190

2.24 Quality Management Plan: Salesforce CPQ 192

2.25 Quality Metrics: Salesforce CPQ 194

2.26 Process Improvement Plan: Salesforce CPQ 196

2.27 Responsibility Assignment Matrix: Salesforce CPQ 198

2.28 Roles and Responsibilities: Salesforce CPQ 200

2.29 Human Resource Management Plan: Salesforce CPQ202

2.30 Communications Management Plan: Salesforce CPQ204

2.31 Risk Management Plan: Salesforce CPQ 206

2.32 Risk Register: Salesforce CPQ 208

2.33 Probability and Impact Assessment: Salesforce CPQ 210

2.34 Probability and Impact Matrix: Salesforce CPQ 212

2.35 Risk Data Sheet: Salesforce CPQ 214

2.36 Procurement Management Plan: Salesforce CPQ 216

2.37 Source Selection Criteria: Salesforce CPQ 218

2.38 Stakeholder Management Plan: Salesforce CPQ 220

2.39 Change Management Plan: Salesforce CPQ 222

3.0 Executing Process Group: Salesforce CPQ 224

3.1 Team Member Status Report: Salesforce CPQ 226

3.2 Change Request: Salesforce CPQ 228

3.3 Change Log: Salesforce CPQ 230

3.4 Decision Log: Salesforce CPQ 232

3.5 Quality Audit: Salesforce CPQ 234

3.6 Team Directory: Salesforce CPQ 237

3.7 Team Operating Agreement: Salesforce CPQ 239

3.8 Team Performance Assessment: Salesforce CPQ 241

3.9 Team Member Performance Assessment: Salesforce CPQ 243

3.10 Issue Log: Salesforce CPQ 245

4.0 Monitoring and Controlling Process Group: Salesforce CPQ 247

4.1 Project Performance Report: Salesforce CPQ 249

4.2 Variance Analysis: Salesforce CPQ 251

4.3 Earned Value Status: Salesforce CPQ 253

4.4 Risk Audit: Salesforce CPQ 255

4.5 Contractor Status Report: Salesforce CPQ 257

4.6 Formal Acceptance: Salesforce CPQ 259

5.0 Closing Process Group: Salesforce CPQ 261

5.1 Procurement Audit: Salesforce CPQ 263

5.2 Contract Close-Out: Salesforce CPQ 266

5.3 Project or Phase Close-Out: Salesforce CPQ 268

5.4 Lessons Learned: Salesforce CPQ 270

Index 272

About The Art of Service

The Art of Service, Business Process Architects since 2000, is dedicated to helping stakeholders achieve excellence.

Defining, designing, creating, and implementing a process to solve a stakeholders challenge or meet an objective is the most valuable role... In EVERY group, company, organization and department.

Unless you're talking a one-time, single-use project, there should be a process. Whether that process is managed and implemented by humans, AI, or a combination of the two, it needs to be designed by someone with a complex enough perspective to ask the right questions.

Someone capable of asking the right questions and step back and say, 'What are we really trying to accomplish here? And is there a different way to look at it?'

With The Art of Service's Self-Assessments, we empower people who can do just that — whether their title is marketer, entrepreneur, manager, salesperson, consultant, Business Process Manager, executive assistant, IT Manager, CIO etc... —they are the people who rule the future. They are people who watch the process as it happens, and ask the right questions to make the process work better.

Contact us when you need any support with this Self-Assessment and any help with templates, blue-prints and examples of standard documents you might need:

https://theartofservice.com
support@theartofservice.com

Included Resources - how to access

Included with your purchase of the book is the Salesforce

CPQ Self-Assessment Spreadsheet Dashboard which contains all questions and Self-Assessment areas and auto-generates insights, graphs, and project RACI planning - all with examples to get you started right away.

How? Simply send an email to
access@theartofservice.com
with this books' title in the subject to get the Salesforce CPQ Self Assessment Tool right away.

The auto reply will guide you further, you will then receive the following contents with New and Updated specific criteria:

- The latest quick edition of the book in PDF
- The latest complete edition of the book in PDF, which criteria correspond to the criteria in...
- The Self-Assessment Excel Dashboard, and...
- Example pre-filled Self-Assessment Excel Dashboard to get familiar with results generation
- In-depth specific Checklists covering the topic
- Project management checklists and templates to assist with implementation

INCLUDES LIFETIME SELF ASSESSMENT UPDATES

Every self assessment comes with Lifetime Updates and Lifetime Free Updated Books. Lifetime Updates is an industry-first feature which allows you to receive verified self assessment updates, ensuring you always have the most accurate information at your fingertips.

Get it now- you will be glad you did - do it now, before you forget.

Send an email to **access@theartofservice.com** with this books' title in the subject to get the Salesforce CPQ Self Assessment Tool right away.

Purpose of this Self-Assessment

This Self-Assessment has been developed to improve understanding of the requirements and elements of Salesforce CPQ, based on best practices and standards in business process architecture, design and quality management.

It is designed to allow for a rapid Self-Assessment to determine how closely existing management practices and procedures correspond to the elements of the Self-Assessment.

The criteria of requirements and elements of Salesforce CPQ have been rephrased in the format of a Self-Assessment questionnaire, with a seven-criterion scoring system, as explained in this document.

In this format, even with limited background knowledge of Salesforce CPQ, a manager can quickly review existing operations to determine how they measure up to the standards. This in turn can serve as the starting point of a 'gap analysis' to identify management tools or system elements that might usefully be implemented in the organization to help improve overall performance.

How to use the Self-Assessment

On the following pages are a series of questions to identify to what extent your Salesforce CPQ initiative is complete in comparison to the requirements set in standards.

To facilitate answering the questions, there is a space in front of each question to enter a score on a scale of '1' to '5'.

1 Strongly Disagree

2 Disagree

3 Neutral

4 Agree

5 Strongly Agree

Read the question and rate it with the following in front of mind:

**'In my belief,
the answer to this question is clearly defined'.**

There are two ways in which you can choose to interpret this statement;

1. how aware are you that the answer to the question is clearly defined
2. for more in-depth analysis you can choose to gather evidence and confirm the answer to the question. This obviously will take more time, most Self-Assessment users opt for the first way to interpret the question and dig deeper later on based on the outcome of the overall Self-Assessment.

A score of '1' would mean that the answer is not clear at all, where a '5' would mean the answer is crystal clear and defined. Leave emtpy when the question is not applicable or you don't want to answer it, you can skip it without affecting your score. Write your score in the space provided.

After you have responded to all the appropriate statements in each section, compute your average score for that section, using the formula provided, and round to the nearest tenth. Then transfer to the corresponding spoke in the Salesforce CPQ Scorecard on the second next page of the Self-Assessment.

Your completed Salesforce CPQ Scorecard will give you a clear presentation of which Salesforce CPQ areas need attention.

Salesforce CPQ Scorecard Example

Example of how the finalized Scorecard can look like:

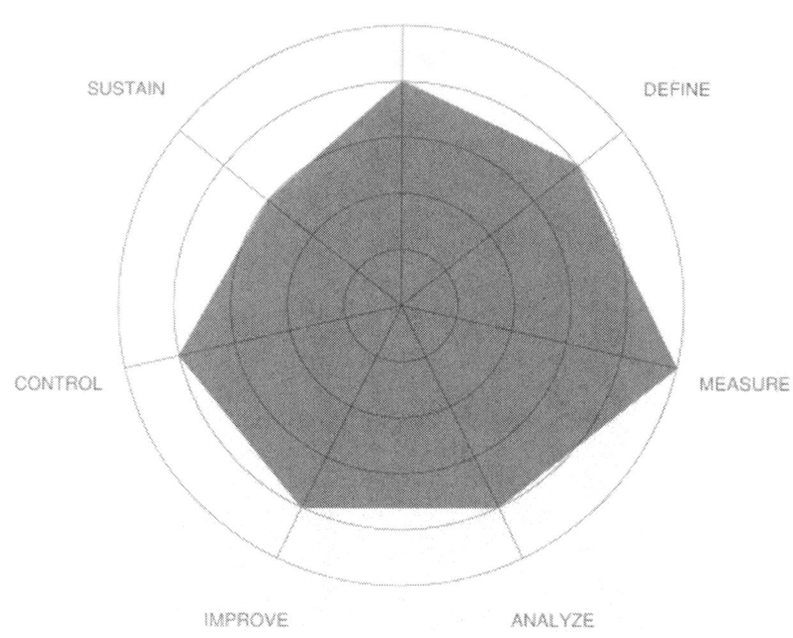

Salesforce CPQ Scorecard

Your Scores:

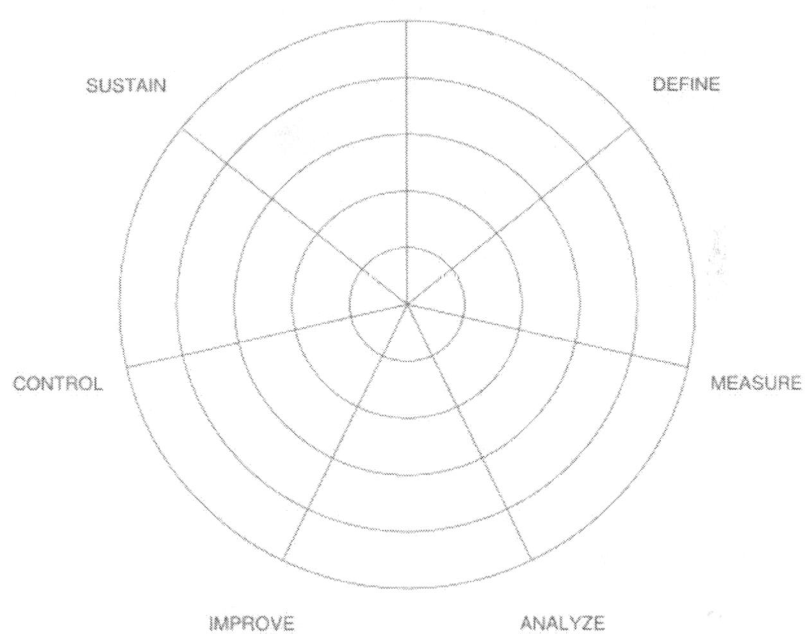

BEGINNING OF THE SELF-ASSESSMENT:

CRITERION #1: RECOGNIZE

INTENT: Be aware of the need for change. Recognize that there is an unfavorable variation, problem or symptom.

In my belief, the answer to this question is clearly defined:

5 Strongly Agree

4 Agree

3 Neutral

2 Disagree

1 Strongly Disagree

1. How much are sponsors, customers, partners, stakeholders involved in Salesforce CPQ? In other words, what are the risks, if Salesforce CPQ does not deliver successfully?
<--- Score

2. Will it solve real problems?
<--- Score

3. Do your users have many tasks or events that are all the same?
<--- Score

4. Which departments or business teams need to be involved?
<--- Score

5. How do you take a forward-looking perspective in identifying Salesforce CPQ research related to market response and models?
<--- Score

6. What situation(s) led to this Salesforce CPQ Self Assessment?
<--- Score

7. Does your customer just need an order status?
<--- Score

8. What Salesforce CPQ events should you attend?
<--- Score

9. What would happen if Salesforce CPQ weren't done?
<--- Score

10. How are you going to measure success?
<--- Score

11. Do organizations need to be located within the same geographic area?
<--- Score

12. What is visual CPQ and why do you need it?
<--- Score

13. What are the expected benefits of Salesforce CPQ to the stakeholder?
<--- Score

14. What type of licence is needed, and who will pay for?
<--- Score

15. Does it accommodate the way you need to work?
<--- Score

16. What would you do if a partner organization is no longer needed and the access of all users needs to be removed?
<--- Score

17. Have you identified your Salesforce CPQ key performance indicators?
<--- Score

18. What is a sign that your organization needs a packaged CPQ tool?
<--- Score

19. How was the account used for the source of transferred funds identified?
<--- Score

20. What type of licence is needed, and who will pay for corresponding?
<--- Score

21. Do you always need help with any of tasks?
<--- Score

22. What do you need your pricing technology to do?
<--- Score

23. Does Salesforce CPQ create potential expectations in other areas that need to be recognized and considered?
<--- Score

24. Are you going to need Pricing for eCommerce?
<--- Score

25. Does the sales team have the information it needs to close deals?
<--- Score

26. What does Salesforce CPQ success mean to the stakeholders?
<--- Score

27. How suitable do you find your current methods to meet your design needs?
<--- Score

28. What needs to be commissioned and how are systems commissioned?
<--- Score

29. Do the suppliers staff meet the expectations and needs of the project?
<--- Score

30. Do you recognize sales challenges?
<--- Score

31. Will a response program recognize when a crisis occurs and provide some level of response?
<--- Score

32. As a sponsor, customer or management, how important is it to meet goals, objectives?
<--- Score

33. What needs to stay?
<--- Score

34. What financial burn will be needed for up-keeping of the software and, yearly operational expenses?
<--- Score

35. Who else hopes to benefit from it?
<--- Score

36. Are configuration control tools used for status accounting and configuration identification tracking?
<--- Score

37. What are your needs in relation to Salesforce CPQ skills, labor, equipment, and markets?
<--- Score

38. Do you identify options that would deliver a more suitable balance?
<--- Score

39. What action do customers need to take?
<--- Score

40. What criteria translate to a critical need for

CPQ?
<--- Score

41. What problems are you facing and how do you consider Salesforce CPQ will circumvent those obstacles?
<--- Score

42. Are there any specific expectations or concerns about the Salesforce CPQ team, Salesforce CPQ itself?
<--- Score

43. What else needs to be measured?
<--- Score

44. How much do you spend on fixing problems when products are delivered with the wrong configuration?
<--- Score

45. What are the stakeholder objectives to be achieved with Salesforce CPQ?
<--- Score

46. Why are you having communication problems?
<--- Score

47. What is your response time to the identification of new viruses and attacks?
<--- Score

48. How are the Salesforce CPQ's objectives aligned to the group's overall stakeholder strategy?
<--- Score

49. Consider your own Salesforce CPQ project, what

types of organizational problems do you think might be causing or affecting your problem, based on the work done so far?
<--- Score

50. What training and capacity building actions are needed to implement proposed reforms?
<--- Score

51. What should be considered when identifying available resources, constraints, and deadlines?
<--- Score

52. What involvement is needed from the business units that you support?
<--- Score

53. Are you seeing an issue regarding compliance rates with certain tags?
<--- Score

54. What are the minority interests and what amount of minority interests can be recognized?
<--- Score

55. For your Salesforce CPQ project, identify and describe the business environment, is there more than one layer to the business environment?
<--- Score

56. What Salesforce CPQ coordination do you need?
<--- Score

57. What are the Salesforce CPQ resources needed?
<--- Score

58. Do you have your organization need to use flows outside of a console app?
<--- Score

Add up total points for this section:
_____ = Total points for this section

Divided by: ______ (number of statements answered) = ______
Average score for this section

Transfer your score to the Salesforce CPQ Index at the beginning of the Self-Assessment.

CRITERION #2: DEFINE:

INTENT: Formulate the stakeholder problem. Define the problem, needs and objectives.

In my belief, the answer to this question is clearly defined:

5 Strongly Agree

4 Agree

3 Neutral

2 Disagree

1 Strongly Disagree

1. How was the 'as is' process map developed, reviewed, verified and validated?
<--- Score

2. Are interfaces or is integration required?
<--- Score

3. Has/have the customer(s) been identified?
<--- Score

4. Is additional hardware or software required?
<--- Score

5. Have you provided a description of your vision, strategy and service culture with regard to the type of services falling within the scope of the contract?
<--- Score

6. Does your organization have a recurring IT requirement?
<--- Score

7. Are customer requirements reviewed and determined prior to submission of a quotation or acceptance of an order?
<--- Score

8. When are meeting minutes sent out? Who is on the distribution list?
<--- Score

9. When is the estimated completion date?
<--- Score

10. Are team charters developed?
<--- Score

11. What are the Roles and Responsibilities for each team member and its leadership? Where is this documented?
<--- Score

12. Has the Salesforce CPQ work been fairly and/or equitably divided and delegated among team

members who are qualified and capable to perform the work? Has everyone contributed?
<--- Score

13. How often are the team meetings?
<--- Score

14. What is the market price of a specific product in a defined geography?
<--- Score

15. Will team members perform Salesforce CPQ work when assigned and in a timely fashion?
<--- Score

16. What is the scope of the Salesforce CPQ effort?
<--- Score

17. How is the team tracking and documenting its work?
<--- Score

18. Is the Salesforce CPQ scope manageable?
<--- Score

19. Are different versions of process maps needed to account for the different types of inputs?
<--- Score

20. Is full participation by members in regularly held team meetings guaranteed?
<--- Score

21. Has the improvement team collected the 'voice of the customer' (obtained feedback – qualitative and quantitative)?

<--- Score

22. Does sales transformation require an investment?
<--- Score

23. Which user permissions does shield platform encryption require?
<--- Score

24. Are stakeholder processes mapped?
<--- Score

25. Is the team sponsored by a champion or stakeholder leader?
<--- Score

26. What constraints exist that might impact the team?
<--- Score

27. How does the Salesforce CPQ manager ensure against scope creep?
<--- Score

28. What knowledge or experience is required?
<--- Score

29. Will team members regularly document their Salesforce CPQ work?
<--- Score

30. What specifically is the problem? Where does it occur? When does it occur? What is its extent?
<--- Score

31. Will professional engineering services be required?
<--- Score

32. Is there a completed, verified, and validated high-level 'as is' (not 'should be' or 'could be') stakeholder process map?
<--- Score

33. Is there regularly 100% attendance at the team meetings? If not, have appointed substitutes attended to preserve cross-functionality and full representation?
<--- Score

34. How and when will the baselines be defined?
<--- Score

35. Is Salesforce CPQ currently on schedule according to the plan?
<--- Score

36. Has a project plan, Gantt chart, or similar been developed/completed?
<--- Score

37. What are the dynamics of the communication plan?
<--- Score

38. Has a high-level 'as is' process map been completed, verified and validated?
<--- Score

39. How did the Salesforce CPQ manager receive input to the development of a Salesforce CPQ

improvement plan and the estimated completion dates/times of each activity?
<--- Score

40. What customer feedback methods were used to solicit their input?
<--- Score

41. Are improvement team members fully trained on Salesforce CPQ?
<--- Score

42. Is special Salesforce CPQ user knowledge required?
<--- Score

43. Are there different segments of customers?
<--- Score

44. How do you manage unclear Salesforce CPQ requirements?
<--- Score

45. When is/was the Salesforce CPQ start date?
<--- Score

46. How do you keep key subject matter experts in the loop?
<--- Score

47. Do you have a Salesforce CPQ success story or case study ready to tell and share?
<--- Score

48. Has a team charter been developed and communicated?

<--- Score

49. What software ecosystems are in use in the case organization?
<--- Score

50. How will variation in the actual durations of each activity be dealt with to ensure that the expected Salesforce CPQ results are met?
<--- Score

51. Is there a completed SIPOC representation, describing the Suppliers, Inputs, Process, Outputs, and Customers?
<--- Score

52. Has the direction changed at all during the course of Salesforce CPQ? If so, when did it change and why?
<--- Score

53. Do you have technical resources available if integration or custom coding is required?
<--- Score

54. Is the team equipped with available and reliable resources?
<--- Score

55. Will your project require a mixing zone?
<--- Score

56. How have you defined all Salesforce CPQ requirements first?
<--- Score

57. What key stakeholder process output measure(s)

does Salesforce CPQ leverage and how?
<--- Score

58. Are customer(s) identified and segmented according to their different needs and requirements?
<--- Score

59. Do you have customers with complex category requirements?
<--- Score

60. Who are the Salesforce CPQ improvement team members, including Management Leads and Coaches?
<--- Score

61. Do the problem and goal statements meet the SMART criteria (specific, measurable, attainable, relevant, and time-bound)?
<--- Score

62. What would be the goal or target for a Salesforce CPQ's improvement team?
<--- Score

63. Are customers identified and high impact areas defined?
<--- Score

64. If substitutes have been appointed, have they been briefed on the Salesforce CPQ goals and received regular communications as to the progress to date?
<--- Score

65. Will your organization make fingerprint

facilities available if required by an Authorized User?
<--- Score

66. Is Salesforce CPQ required?
<--- Score

67. Is the team adequately staffed with the desired cross-functionality? If not, what additional resources are available to the team?
<--- Score

68. What are the record-keeping requirements of Salesforce CPQ activities?
<--- Score

69. How difficult is it for you to keep working on projects that require more than a few months to complete?
<--- Score

70. How do you access predefined profile options?
<--- Score

71. Has a Salesforce CPQ requirement not been met?
<--- Score

72. Is a fully trained team formed, supported, and committed to work on the Salesforce CPQ improvements?
<--- Score

73. Is there a Salesforce CPQ management charter, including stakeholder case, problem and goal statements, scope, milestones, roles and responsibilities, communication plan?

<--- Score

74. What scope to assess?
<--- Score

75. Has your scope been defined?
<--- Score

76. How were the requirements created?
<--- Score

77. What are the Salesforce CPQ tasks and definitions?
<--- Score

78. What are the compelling stakeholder reasons for embarking on Salesforce CPQ?
<--- Score

79. Has anyone else (internal or external to the group) attempted to solve this problem or a similar one before? If so, what knowledge can be leveraged from these previous efforts?
<--- Score

80. Is the work to date meeting requirements?
<--- Score

81. What are the rough order estimates on cost savings/opportunities that Salesforce CPQ brings?
<--- Score

82. Are upgrade releases compulsory or can a customer remain on a previous version of the software if required?
<--- Score

83. Are there any constraints known that bear on the ability to perform Salesforce CPQ work? How is the team addressing them?
<--- Score

84. Does the team have regular meetings?
<--- Score

85. What types of redundant services are required?
<--- Score

86. Is your application deployed solely via a browser, or is a client installation recommended or required?
<--- Score

87. Do you sell complex products that require customized pricing and specific rules?
<--- Score

88. Have the customer needs been translated into specific, measurable requirements? How?
<--- Score

89. Who defines (or who defined) the rules and roles?
<--- Score

90. Will selected vendor resources be required to perform off-hours, on-call support?
<--- Score

91. Are the requirements Preferred or Must Have?
<--- Score

92. Is the team formed and are team leaders (Coaches and Management Leads) assigned?

<--- Score

93. What is a worst-case scenario for losses?
<--- Score

94. Is data collected and displayed to better understand customer(s) critical needs and requirements.
<--- Score

95. What critical content must be communicated – who, what, when, where, and how?
<--- Score

96. Is there a critical path to deliver Salesforce CPQ results?
<--- Score

97. What information is required in addition to CPQ?
<--- Score

98. What types of information must be gathered about each corporate location?
<--- Score

99. Is the current 'as is' process being followed? If not, what are the discrepancies?
<--- Score

100. How will the Salesforce CPQ team and the group measure complete success of Salesforce CPQ?
<--- Score

101. Are there any requirements or restrictions on use of funds for the place-based track?

<--- Score

102. Is the improvement team aware of the different versions of a process: what they think it is vs. what it actually is vs. what it should be vs. what it could be?
<--- Score

103. Is your organization license required?
<--- Score

104. Are audit criteria, scope, frequency and methods defined?
<--- Score

105. Does part of your online sales experience require configurable products and prices?
<--- Score

106. Is Salesforce CPQ linked to key stakeholder goals and objectives?
<--- Score

107. How are software ecosystems utilized in the case organization?
<--- Score

108. What hardware and software resources are required?
<--- Score

109. What are the boundaries of the scope? What is in bounds and what is not? What is the start point? What is the stop point?
<--- Score

110. Has everyone on the team, including the team

leaders, been properly trained?
<--- Score

111. How do you manage hot leads that require an immediate quote?
<--- Score

112. Is your organization required to complete?
<--- Score

Add up total points for this section:
_____ = Total points for this section

Divided by: ______ (number of statements answered) = ______ Average score for this section

Transfer your score to the Salesforce CPQ Index at the beginning of the Self-Assessment.

CRITERION #3: MEASURE:

INTENT: Gather the correct data.
Measure the current performance and
evolution of the situation.

In my belief, the answer to this
question is clearly defined:

5 Strongly Agree

4 Agree

3 Neutral

2 Disagree

1 Strongly Disagree

1. What are the relative costs of a solution?
<--- Score

2. How is data to be captured, stored, analyzed and passed on?
<--- Score

3. Is data collection planned and executed?
<--- Score

4. What is the significance of process and product in the network analysis and design methodology?
<--- Score

5. Was a data collection plan established?
<--- Score

6. Do the benefits outweigh the costs?
<--- Score

7. How long to keep data and how to manage retention costs?
<--- Score

8. Do charter organizations improve employee achievement?
<--- Score

9. Will all the benefits of mandatory fortification outweigh all the costs?
<--- Score

10. Which services will be most impacted by technology?
<--- Score

11. Have you found any 'ground fruit' or 'low-hanging fruit' for immediate remedies to the gap in performance?
<--- Score

12. What are the agreed upon definitions of the high impact areas, defect(s), unit(s), and opportunities that will figure into the process capability metrics?
<--- Score

13. How large is the gap between current performance and the customer-specified (goal) performance?
<--- Score

14. Is there an opportunity to verify requirements?
<--- Score

15. Is it increased flexibility, reduced cost, more satisfied business users?
<--- Score

16. What kind of analytics data will be gathered?
<--- Score

17. Do your sales teams make costing and pricing errors?
<--- Score

18. What are predictive Salesforce CPQ analytics?
<--- Score

19. Do you struggle to manage person accounts because your sales team unknowingly creates duplicates?
<--- Score

20. Who participated in the data collection for measurements?
<--- Score

21. How will you manage time and resources spent on reporting and deep-dive analysis?
<--- Score

22. Which entities create components and who is focused on systems?
<--- Score

23. Where should executives spend scarce resources to get the most profit impact for investment?
<--- Score

24. Does Salesforce CPQ analysis isolate the fundamental causes of problems?
<--- Score

25. Is it cost effective to collect and report the data?
<--- Score

26. Will all the benefits of increased voluntary fortification outweigh all the costs?
<--- Score

27. Is a solid data collection plan established that includes measurement systems analysis?
<--- Score

28. Are expenditure entries posted by cost centers?
<--- Score

29. How do you continue to cut costs and drive efficiencies while simultaneously gearing up to grow the business and increase agility?
<--- Score

30. What is the difference between total cost of ownership and total benefit of ownership to your

organization?
<--- Score

31. What is your highest priority for improving the configure-price-quote process?
<--- Score

32. How frequently do you verify your Salesforce CPQ strategy?
<--- Score

33. Do you effectively measure and reward individual and team performance?
<--- Score

34. Do staff have the necessary skills to collect, analyze, and report data?
<--- Score

35. Do you want a Configure, Price and Quote system that delivers exceptional business results while keeping control of your ongoing costs?
<--- Score

36. What data do you view from the white space analysis report?
<--- Score

37. What are allowable costs?
<--- Score

38. Why are some environments better than others for charter organizations?
<--- Score

39. What is the Salesforce CPQ business impact?

<--- Score

40. How do you use different representations to analyze linear functions?
<--- Score

41. What data was collected (past, present, future/ ongoing)?
<--- Score

42. Are process variation components displayed/ communicated using suitable charts, graphs, plots?
<--- Score

43. Is there a Performance Baseline?
<--- Score

44. Is data collected on key measures that were identified?
<--- Score

45. What impact does the solution have on your business/mission?
<--- Score

46. What users will be impacted?
<--- Score

47. How will you measure success?
<--- Score

48. How do you improve cost of ownership?
<--- Score

49. Are losses documented, analyzed, and remedial processes developed to prevent future losses?

<--- Score

50. What is the impact of your competitors on your sales?
<--- Score

51. Does the solution automate call and email routing to support prioritization and reduce wait times?
<--- Score

52. How do you verify and validate the Salesforce CPQ data?
<--- Score

53. Are key measures identified and agreed upon?
<--- Score

54. Is your organization investing in Dark Data Analytics?
<--- Score

55. Is key measure data collection planned and executed, process variation displayed and communicated and performance baselined?
<--- Score

56. What does a Test Case verify?
<--- Score

57. Which measures and indicators matter?
<--- Score

58. What is the benefit/ impact for the buyer?
<--- Score

59. What key measures identified indicate the performance of the stakeholder process?
<--- Score

60. Do visual additions to CPQ make a difference to the bottom line, and at what cost?
<--- Score

61. What are the impacts of alternatives on quality criteria?
<--- Score

62. Will implementation impact other IT projects?
<--- Score

63. What particular quality tools did the team find helpful in establishing measurements?
<--- Score

64. Is it possible to estimate the impact of unanticipated complexity such as wrong or failed assumptions, feedback, etcetera on proposed reforms?
<--- Score

65. What could cause delays in the schedule?
<--- Score

66. What do you measure and why?
<--- Score

67. Have you made assumptions about the shape of the future, particularly its impact on your customers and competitors?
<--- Score

68. Is there any impact on branch mobility during WAN failures?
<--- Score

69. Does management have the right priorities among projects?
<--- Score

70. What happens when you click a recommendation from the white space analysis report?
<--- Score

71. What charts has the team used to display the components of variation in the process?
<--- Score

72. How long have employees been focused without an opportunity to interact?
<--- Score

73. How much will making the change cost in additional project costs?
<--- Score

74. How will the new era of transparency impact B2B selling and how does your organization use it to your advantage?
<--- Score

75. How do you prevent mis-estimating cost?
<--- Score

76. What are the operational costs after Salesforce CPQ deployment?
<--- Score

77. How do you verify your imported data?
<--- Score

78. What does your operating model cost?
<--- Score

79. What factors are impacting your sales teams performance?
<--- Score

80. What are the key input variables? What are the key process variables? What are the key output variables?
<--- Score

81. Is Process Variation Displayed/Communicated?
<--- Score

82. Have design-to-cost goals been established?
<--- Score

83. What has the team done to assure the stability and accuracy of the measurement process?
<--- Score

84. What risk-free rate do you recommend be used as a proxy for the risk-free rate in the current analysis?
<--- Score

85. Are Salesforce CPQ vulnerabilities categorized and prioritized?
<--- Score

86. What are you verifying?
<--- Score

87. Are high impact defects defined and identified in the stakeholder process?
<--- Score

88. What impact will CPQ make on roles, and your need for resources?
<--- Score

89. Can services be offered remotely to help further reduce cost?
<--- Score

90. What would the impacts of options be on your business?
<--- Score

91. Is long term and short term variability accounted for?
<--- Score

Add up total points for this section:
_____ = Total points for this section

Divided by: ______ (number of statements answered) = ______ Average score for this section

Transfer your score to the Salesforce CPQ Index at the beginning of the Self-Assessment.

CRITERION #4: ANALYZE:

INTENT: Analyze causes, assumptions and hypotheses.

In my belief, the answer to this question is clearly defined:

5 Strongly Agree

4 Agree

3 Neutral

2 Disagree

1 Strongly Disagree

1. What are the Salesforce CPQ design outputs?
<--- Score

2. Do your processes tend to exclude possible suppliers, as smaller operators?
<--- Score

3. Do you have a documented process for configuring products, pricing and quoting today?
<--- Score

4. Which process was allegedly deviated from?
<--- Score

5. How do you summarize, represent, and interpret data on a single count or measurement variable?
<--- Score

6. Do you choose where your data is stored?
<--- Score

7. What quality tools were used to get through the analyze phase?
<--- Score

8. How will the data be checked for quality?
<--- Score

9. How do you change your primary contact in an opportunity, account, or lead?
<--- Score

10. Do you collect the right kinds of data?
<--- Score

11. Who will facilitate the team and process?
<--- Score

12. What record of searches will be left on the databases?
<--- Score

13. Who will gather what data?
<--- Score

14. How can confidence in data and underlying

disclosures be increased?
<--- Score

15. What is the escalation process for critical issues?
<--- Score

16. Does your sales force really need more contact data?
<--- Score

17. Why is it that opportunities always look bigger going than coming?
<--- Score

18. What Salesforce CPQ data should be managed?
<--- Score

19. Who is primarily responsible for maintaining and handling your due diligence process?
<--- Score

20. Were Pareto charts (or similar) used to portray the 'heavy hitters' (or key sources of variation)?
<--- Score

21. How do you convert prospects to accounts, what is the process flow?
<--- Score

22. What tools were used to narrow the list of possible causes?
<--- Score

23. Is the data used for the metric accurate and reliable?

<--- Score

24. How can information management help in making the quotation process more transparent?
<--- Score

25. What does each stage in the CPQ process entail?
<--- Score

26. How to find, assess and value open innovation opportunities by leveraging IP databases?
<--- Score

27. What did the team gain from developing a sub-process map?
<--- Score

28. Did any additional data need to be collected?
<--- Score

29. What systems/processes must you excel at?
<--- Score

30. What is a billing account on an opportunity?
<--- Score

31. How do you remove a contact from an opportunity, account, or lead?
<--- Score

32. How is warranty billed, what approval process from manufacturer must be completed before certified warranty repair takes place?
<--- Score

33. Were there any improvement opportunities identified from the process analysis?
<--- Score

34. Is your data structure designed for maximum success?
<--- Score

35. What is the difference between sales methodology and sales process?
<--- Score

36. How does the process work at that point?
<--- Score

37. What information is required to create an opportunity?
<--- Score

38. How is the way you as the leader think and process information affecting your organizational culture?
<--- Score

39. Do you sort opportunity searches by the last update date?
<--- Score

40. How would you rate aspects of your current configure-price-quote process/system?
<--- Score

41. What database is used for the message store?
<--- Score

42. Have any additional benefits been identified that will result from closing all or most of the gaps?

<--- Score

43. Is the size of your dataset slowing you down?
<--- Score

44. Are gaps between current performance and the goal performance identified?
<--- Score

45. How can consumer data be used in marketing?
<--- Score

46. Why is workforce data important?
<--- Score

47. How was the detailed process map generated, verified, and validated?
<--- Score

48. What is your sales process & structure to-be based on your organizational strategy and roadmap?
<--- Score

49. Are there opportunities to review and improve data collection systems in a participatory way?
<--- Score

50. What benefits you foresee for your business by moving the CPQ process on to cloud?
<--- Score

51. What do you need to qualify?
<--- Score

52. What level of data do you see in order to drive

suitable offers being made?
<--- Score

53. How will corresponding data be collected?
<--- Score

54. Was a detailed process map created to amplify critical steps of the 'as is' stakeholder process?
<--- Score

55. What are process input conditions?
<--- Score

56. Were any designed experiments used to generate additional insight into the data analysis?
<--- Score

57. Which output is allowed for business transactions?
<--- Score

58. How are you moving that vital customer and order data from system to system?
<--- Score

59. Is there any way to speed up the process?
<--- Score

60. Are there charges for integrating applications and data sources?
<--- Score

61. What if you want to use your own hashing process to hash your tenant secret?
<--- Score

62. How sophisticated is the use of the data?
<--- Score

63. What is the benefit of digitizing sales processes with CPQ?
<--- Score

64. Is the Salesforce CPQ process severely broken such that a re-design is necessary?
<--- Score

65. What are the processes for audit reporting and management?
<--- Score

66. Does the solution come with functionality to automate prospect outreach and lead qualification?
<--- Score

67. Is the gap/opportunity displayed and communicated in financial terms?
<--- Score

68. What were the financial benefits resulting from any 'ground fruit or low-hanging fruit' (quick fixes)?
<--- Score

69. What about the application process?
<--- Score

70. How organizations are using AI marketing to drive innovation and create new growth areas?
<--- Score

71. Is there a charge if you choose to relocate your

data?
<--- Score

72. What are the key areas to look out for as you go through an upgrade process?
<--- Score

73. Have you defined which data is gathered how?
<--- Score

74. Is the performance gap determined?
<--- Score

75. How do you navigate organizational politics to drive your pricing philosophy?
<--- Score

76. How do you assign team members automatically to an opportunity?
<--- Score

77. What relationships will the classification scheme have with system processes?
<--- Score

78. Think about some of the processes you undertake within your organization, which do you own?
<--- Score

79. What data & relationships do you need to move policy forward?
<--- Score

80. What conclusions were drawn from the team's data collection and analysis? How did the team reach these conclusions?

<--- Score

81. When should a process be art not science?
<--- Score

82. Do you create more than one opportunity from a single lead?
<--- Score

83. How are territories assigned to opportunities?
<--- Score

84. What detective or predictive reports can determine fraudulent data?
<--- Score

85. Did any value-added analysis or 'lean thinking' take place to identify some of the gaps shown on the 'as is' process map?
<--- Score

86. What is typically wrong with a CPQ process in high tech?
<--- Score

87. How do you synchronize your offline data?
<--- Score

88. What is the process for adding sub-contractors?
<--- Score

89. Does your CPQ solution have guided buying and selling processes?
<--- Score

90. What is the decision-making process?
<--- Score

91. Do you make instructional decisions and adaptations based on your employees data?
<--- Score

92. How is the expected close date of an opportunity initially set?
<--- Score

93. What should your new processes look like?
<--- Score

94. Where are the gaps in your knowledge, data, perspective or services?
<--- Score

95. What were the crucial 'moments of truth' on the process map?
<--- Score

96. What is the cost of poor quality as supported by the team's analysis?
<--- Score

97. What data needs to be integrated regularly?
<--- Score

98. How effective is your pricing process?
<--- Score

99. What interfaces are supported for data and reporting integrations?
<--- Score

100. What processes, tools, or systems do you use as part of your current workflow?
<--- Score

101. How is data used for program management and improvement?
<--- Score

102. What data are you and the other organization allowed to use?
<--- Score

103. What if your data changes with the seasons?
<--- Score

104. What would happen today if a disaster hit your data center?
<--- Score

105. Are there additional elements that are important for regulators to understand beyond the categories of quote/order originator, price, size and time of the order (e.g., inventory or position data)?
<--- Score

106. Who will check the data is being captured?
<--- Score

107. What does the data say about the performance of the stakeholder process?
<--- Score

108. What are the difficulties in transporting voice and data simultaneously?
<--- Score

109. What are the revised rough estimates of the financial savings/opportunity for Salesforce CPQ improvements?
<--- Score

110. Is data and process analysis, root cause analysis and quantifying the gap/opportunity in place?
<--- Score

111. What other organizational variables, such as reward systems or communication systems, affect the performance of this Salesforce CPQ process?
<--- Score

112. How does the solution drive sales productivity?
<--- Score

113. Was a cause-and-effect diagram used to explore the different types of causes (or sources of variation)?
<--- Score

114. Is workflow and complex API-driven processing required?
<--- Score

115. Are there additional charges for batch transaction processing?
<--- Score

116. Are opportunities missed when service contracts expire or products age out and should be replaced or updated?
<--- Score

117. Is the data clean and error-free?
<--- Score

118. What happens if your organization has been sharing positive data and now considers that it is no longer appropriate to do so?
<--- Score

119. What data are needed to use money wisely?
<--- Score

120. Is the data integration rule mapping for updating records missing a field that you want to update?
<--- Score

121. Is your organization expecting vendors to manage/own the process?
<--- Score

122. Have the problem and goal statements been updated to reflect the additional knowledge gained from the analyze phase?
<--- Score

123. Do cases generated outside of regular business hours disrupt your escalation process?
<--- Score

124. What tools were used to generate the list of possible causes?
<--- Score

125. What Salesforce CPQ data will be collected?
<--- Score

Add up total points for this section:
_____ = Total points for this section

Divided by: ______ (number of statements answered) = ______ Average score for this section

Transfer your score to the Salesforce CPQ Index at the beginning of the Self-Assessment.

CRITERION #5: IMPROVE:

INTENT: Develop a practical solution. Innovate, establish and test the solution and to measure the results.

In my belief, the answer to this question is clearly defined:

5 Strongly Agree

4 Agree

3 Neutral

2 Disagree

1 Strongly Disagree

1. Will successful implementation of the research result in system efficiencies?
<--- Score

2. How do risk managers identify risk in your organization as an outcome of ethical behavior?
<--- Score

3. How will the team or the process owner(s) monitor

the implementation plan to see that it is working as intended?
<--- Score

4. What do you personally intend to do differently as a result of the activity?
<--- Score

5. What type of customer support is included with the solution?
<--- Score

6. How do you deal with Salesforce CPQ risk?
<--- Score

7. Is the optimal solution selected based on testing and analysis?
<--- Score

8. How do customers contact the support team, and what SLAs exist for support responses and resolution?
<--- Score

9. Are risk management tasks balanced centrally and locally?
<--- Score

10. Is there a small-scale pilot for proposed improvement(s)? What conclusions were drawn from the outcomes of a pilot?
<--- Score

11. Who are the Salesforce CPQ decision makers?
<--- Score

12. Does the solution auto-populate records and forms?
<--- Score

13. For estimation problems, how do you develop an estimation statement?
<--- Score

14. Does a quote for a customer take days for a sales rep to prepare and sometimes result in lost sales?
<--- Score

15. Is a solution implementation plan established, including schedule/work breakdown structure, resources, risk management plan, cost/budget, and control plan?
<--- Score

16. Will you be carrying out any high risk work?
<--- Score

17. Who controls key decisions that will be made?
<--- Score

18. What suggestions did stakeholders have for improvements?
<--- Score

19. What do you look for when selecting a CPQ solution?
<--- Score

20. How is continuous improvement applied to risk management?
<--- Score

21. Is there any other Salesforce CPQ solution?
<--- Score

22. Who is the CPQ solution designed for?
<--- Score

23. How can you improve Salesforce CPQ?
<--- Score

24. Is your CPQ solution mobile and off-line capable?
<--- Score

25. Does the solution include offline mobile capabilities?
<--- Score

26. Do you have the optimal project management team structure?
<--- Score

27. Are possible solutions generated and tested?
<--- Score

28. Was a pilot designed for the proposed solution(s)?
<--- Score

29. Who are the Salesforce CPQ decision-makers?
<--- Score

30. Are the most efficient solutions problem-specific?
<--- Score

31. How do you request developer support?
<--- Score

32. What assumptions are made about the solution and approach?
<--- Score

33. How often do you provide new releases and maintenance to your solution?
<--- Score

34. What were the underlying assumptions on the cost-benefit analysis?
<--- Score

35. Has it helped you to have a better control over rogue discounting and improve price retention?
<--- Score

36. What does the 'should be' process map/design look like?
<--- Score

37. Will successful implementation of the research result in resource savings?
<--- Score

38. How is knowledge sharing about risk management improved?
<--- Score

39. How does the solution remove the key sources of issues discovered in the analyze phase?
<--- Score

40. Are procedures documented for managing Salesforce CPQ risks?
<--- Score

41. Is your CPQ solution available on a variety of mobile devices?
<--- Score

42. Is there a high likelihood that any recommendations will achieve their intended results?
<--- Score

43. Who do you report Salesforce CPQ results to?
<--- Score

44. Did you understand/interpret your business requirements?
<--- Score

45. What current systems have to be understood and/or changed?
<--- Score

46. Are there any constraints (technical, political, cultural, or otherwise) that would inhibit certain solutions?
<--- Score

47. Does improved financial knowledge actually lead to improved financial capability and behaviors?
<--- Score

48. What communications are necessary to support the implementation of the solution?
<--- Score

49. What is the solution of the equation?
<--- Score

50. What risk shifts do you see in other of corresponding areas?
<--- Score

51. How many quotes are created with the solution?
<--- Score

52. Does the CPQ solution support a mobile workforce?
<--- Score

53. What actually has to improve and by how much?
<--- Score

54. Are improved process ('should be') maps modified based on pilot data and analysis?
<--- Score

55. What error proofing will be done to address some of the discrepancies observed in the 'as is' process?
<--- Score

56. What to do with the results or outcomes of measurements?
<--- Score

57. How did the team generate the list of possible solutions?
<--- Score

58. Is pilot data collected and analyzed?
<--- Score

59. Do you understand your point about the

personal guarantees?
<--- Score

60. Is a contingency plan established?
<--- Score

61. Are you satisfied with the resolution?
<--- Score

62. Where should you look for the right CPQ solution?
<--- Score

63. Is a CPQ solution just for use within sales?
<--- Score

64. Can you integrate quality management and risk management?
<--- Score

65. Does the CPQ solution work on mobile and tablet devices?
<--- Score

66. Which industries benefit from a CPQ solution?
<--- Score

67. What constitutes a good CPQ solution?
<--- Score

68. How is the platform optimized for extensibility and customization?
<--- Score

69. What do you want to improve?
<--- Score

70. What is Salesforce CPQ's impact on utilizing the best solution(s)?
<--- Score

71. How many users use the solution?
<--- Score

72. What is Salesforce CPQ risk?
<--- Score

73. What is the team's contingency plan for potential problems occurring in implementation?
<--- Score

74. How does your organization decide what products and services to market?
<--- Score

75. Is there a cost/benefit analysis of optimal solution(s)?
<--- Score

76. What are the Salesforce CPQ security risks?
<--- Score

77. What level of product bundling resulted in the most efficient contracts?
<--- Score

78. What expertise and tools will you need to customize the solution?
<--- Score

79. How do you link measurement and risk?
<--- Score

80. What lessons, if any, from a pilot were incorporated into the design of the full-scale solution?
<--- Score

81. Are the risks fully understood, reasonable and manageable?
<--- Score

82. Is the solution technically practical?
<--- Score

83. Do you need to do a usability evaluation?
<--- Score

84. How can too much information be as detrimental as too little information for decision makers?
<--- Score

85. Were any criteria developed to assist the team in testing and evaluating potential solutions?
<--- Score

86. Why would shareholders pay a manager to reduce risk if the shareholder can achieve the same effect more easily by diversification?
<--- Score

87. Will successful implementation of the research result in a safety enhancement?
<--- Score

88. Does the solution provide both real time dashboards and historical view reporting?
<--- Score

89. What attendant changes will need to be made to ensure that the solution is successful?
<--- Score

90. How will you know that a change is an improvement?
<--- Score

91. What are the benefits of CPQ solutions?
<--- Score

92. Are staff members asked to review and comment on evaluation?
<--- Score

93. What strategies have you used to improve your writing?
<--- Score

94. What tools were most useful during the improve phase?
<--- Score

95. What tools were used to evaluate the potential solutions?
<--- Score

96. How will a CPQ system deliver measurable results?
<--- Score

97. Does the solution provide access to the full source code?
<--- Score

98. Are new and improved process ('should be') maps developed?
<--- Score

99. What are the possible disadvantages or risks of taking part?
<--- Score

100. Are your salespeople protecting your brand, or putting it at risk with inaccurate or incomplete quotes?
<--- Score

101. Does your solution be deployed in the cloud?
<--- Score

102. Is the implementation plan designed?
<--- Score

103. Is the solution written in a proprietary language?
<--- Score

104. What are the long-term maintenance demands for running the solution?
<--- Score

105. What alternative responses are available to manage risk?
<--- Score

106. Is the Salesforce CPQ solution sustainable?
<--- Score

107. Does your team have room for improvement when it comes to productivity?

<--- Score

108. Does the solution automate workflows?
<--- Score

109. Who understands the benefits of AI?
<--- Score

110. Are the key business and technology risks being managed?
<--- Score

111. Are you currently driving some form of optimized price to the sales team?
<--- Score

112. How do you decide how much to remunerate an employee?
<--- Score

113. How will you receive purchase orders resulting from eQuotes?
<--- Score

114. Can the vendor be trusted to provide business improvements while mitigating risks?
<--- Score

115. Has any organization been so charged, allegedly as a result of any action or conduct on your part?
<--- Score

116. Who manages supplier risk management in your organization?
<--- Score

117. Will the subjects encounter the risk of psychological, social, physical or legal risk?
<--- Score

118. Are the best solutions selected?
<--- Score

119. What is the implementation plan?
<--- Score

120. How do you improve Salesforce CPQ service perception, and satisfaction?
<--- Score

121. What is the solution of the system?
<--- Score

122. Describe the design of the pilot and what tests were conducted, if any?
<--- Score

123. Is Salesforce CPQ documentation maintained?
<--- Score

124. How will the group know that the solution worked?
<--- Score

125. Who will be responsible for making the decisions to include or exclude requested changes once Salesforce CPQ is underway?
<--- Score

126. How easily can a solution be bypassed?
<--- Score

127. What is the risk?
<--- Score

128. How would employees change as a result of peer mediation program involvement?
<--- Score

129. What tools were used to tap into the creativity and encourage 'outside the box' thinking?
<--- Score

130. How can the communication subsystems be utilized optimally?
<--- Score

131. Who makes decisions about resources?
<--- Score

132. Which industries benefit from CPQ visualization Solutions?
<--- Score

133. Can the solution be designed and implemented within an acceptable time period?
<--- Score

134. Who will be using the results of the measurement activities?
<--- Score

Add up total points for this section:
_____ = Total points for this section

Divided by: ______ (number of statements answered) = ______

Average score for this section

Transfer your score to the Salesforce CPQ Index at the beginning of the Self-Assessment.

CRITERION #6: CONTROL:

INTENT: Implement the practical solution. Maintain the performance and correct possible complications.

In my belief, the answer to this question is clearly defined:

5 Strongly Agree

4 Agree

3 Neutral

2 Disagree

1 Strongly Disagree

1. How many potential new Partners are planned for integration?
<--- Score

2. What key inputs and outputs are being measured on an ongoing basis?
<--- Score

3. Does the response plan contain a definite closed

loop continual improvement scheme (e.g., plan-do-check-act)?
<--- Score

4. Can you adapt and adjust to changing Salesforce CPQ situations?
<--- Score

5. Is there a documented and implemented monitoring plan?
<--- Score

6. How does your organization compare to benchmarks or standards?
<--- Score

7. What comes with your premier success plan?
<--- Score

8. Is a response plan established and deployed?
<--- Score

9. Are corresponding explanations acceptable?
<--- Score

10. Will the application perform and scale?
<--- Score

11. Where can customers and prospects learn more?
<--- Score

12. Is there a control plan in place for sustaining improvements (short and long-term)?
<--- Score

13. What are standard and custom objects in salesforce?
<--- Score

14. How will input, process, and output variables be checked to detect for sub-optimal conditions?
<--- Score

15. Are suggested corrective/restorative actions indicated on the response plan for known causes to problems that might surface?
<--- Score

16. What is the best design framework for Salesforce CPQ organization now that, in a post industrial-age if the top-down, command and control model is no longer relevant?
<--- Score

17. How might the group capture best practices and lessons learned so as to leverage improvements?
<--- Score

18. Is there a standardized process?
<--- Score

19. Are operating procedures consistent?
<--- Score

20. What are various ways that employees could demonstrate learning?
<--- Score

21. Who at the administrative level participated in implementation planning?
<--- Score

22. Do you use your existing contracts to standardize on a particular system/brand?
<--- Score

23. What actions, if any, by the end user affect the standard warranty coverage?
<--- Score

24. Who controls critical resources?
<--- Score

25. What were trying to understand is are there - there is standard types of - is there an abuse of market power going on here?
<--- Score

26. How will the day-to-day responsibilities for monitoring and continual improvement be transferred from the improvement team to the process owner?
<--- Score

27. Why is CPQ software essential to organizations looking to scale?
<--- Score

28. Does the Salesforce CPQ performance meet the customer's requirements?
<--- Score

29. What is the skill you want employees to learn?
<--- Score

30. Are there documented procedures?
<--- Score

31. How do you monitor the goods movement?
<--- Score

32. What actions is your organization currently taking or planning to take to accomplish that?
<--- Score

33. What impact does the solution have on standard performance?
<--- Score

34. How will new or emerging customer needs/ requirements be checked/communicated to orient the process toward meeting the new specifications and continually reducing variation?
<--- Score

35. Is there documentation that will support the successful operation of the improvement?
<--- Score

36. What standard reports are included with the system?
<--- Score

37. What are data management, record-keeping and monitoring?
<--- Score

38. Is knowledge gained on process shared and institutionalized?
<--- Score

39. Do the viable solutions scale to future needs?
<--- Score

40. What is the term for multiple products and services in a standardized offering?
<--- Score

41. How are you planning to sell your Products & Services?
<--- Score

42. Is reporting being used or needed?
<--- Score

43. What quality tools were useful in the control phase?
<--- Score

44. What should the next improvement project be that is related to Salesforce CPQ?
<--- Score

45. How does your organization plan to procure project-definition based services?
<--- Score

46. Is a response plan in place for when the input, process, or output measures indicate an 'out-of-control' condition?
<--- Score

47. Should the market monitoring report be brought up again?
<--- Score

48. Who is providing loss control services?
<--- Score

49. Are documented procedures clear and easy to follow for the operators?
<--- Score

50. What other systems, operations, processes, and infrastructures (hiring practices, staffing, training, incentives/rewards, metrics/dashboards/scorecards, etc.) need updates, additions, changes, or deletions in order to facilitate knowledge transfer and improvements?
<--- Score

51. Is there a Salesforce CPQ Communication plan covering who needs to get what information when?
<--- Score

52. What is the plan to integrate CPQ Cloud with Fusion Applications?
<--- Score

53. What if instead of racing against the clock, you could deliver on time, every time?
<--- Score

54. What is the control/monitoring plan?
<--- Score

55. Who is the Salesforce CPQ process owner?
<--- Score

56. Are pertinent alerts monitored, analyzed and distributed to appropriate personnel?
<--- Score

57. Do you have a configuration control board?
<--- Score

58. Is there a transfer of ownership and knowledge to process owner and process team tasked with the responsibilities.
<--- Score

59. What other areas of the group might benefit from the Salesforce CPQ team's improvements, knowledge, and learning?
<--- Score

60. How will the process owner and team be able to hold the gains?
<--- Score

61. Is it able to scale as your organization grows and needs change?
<--- Score

62. Is there a recommended audit plan for routine surveillance inspections of Salesforce CPQ's gains?
<--- Score

63. How will the process owner verify improvement in present and future sigma levels, process capabilities?
<--- Score

64. How do larger, enterprise-scale companies deal with the conflicting needs of Chief Financial Officers and Chief Revenue Officers and/or VPs of Sales?
<--- Score

65. Who has control over resources?
<--- Score

66. Does a troubleshooting guide exist or is it needed?
<--- Score

67. Is there a better, more efficient way to control discounts and pricing approvals?
<--- Score

68. How many majors do you plan to complete?
<--- Score

69. Has the improved process and its steps been standardized?
<--- Score

70. Can there be a plan to balance the noise across all the collar communities?
<--- Score

71. How can spending be measured against performance outcomes or results delivered?
<--- Score

72. What are the critical parameters to watch?
<--- Score

73. Have new or revised work instructions resulted?
<--- Score

74. How likely is the current Salesforce CPQ plan to come in on schedule or on budget?
<--- Score

75. Does job training on the documented procedures need to be part of the process team's education and training?
<--- Score

76. How will report readings be checked to effectively monitor performance?
<--- Score

77. What is the recommended frequency of auditing?
<--- Score

78. Are new process steps, standards, and documentation ingrained into normal operations?
<--- Score

79. Is new knowledge gained imbedded in the response plan?
<--- Score

80. Can support from partners be adjusted?
<--- Score

81. Are the individuals responsible for billing involved in the planning?
<--- Score

82. What costs would be involved in running a large-scale health promotion strategy to increase the folate status of the population?
<--- Score

83. Will any special training be provided for results interpretation?
<--- Score

Add up total points for this section:
_____ = Total points for this section

Divided by: ______ (number of

statements answered) = ______
Average score for this section

Transfer your score to the Salesforce CPQ Index at the beginning of the Self-Assessment.

CRITERION #7: SUSTAIN:

INTENT: Retain the benefits.

In my belief, the answer to this question is clearly defined:

5 Strongly Agree

4 Agree

3 Neutral

2 Disagree

1 Strongly Disagree

1. What is the dollar value of the project/order?
<--- Score

2. Which professions perform what services?
<--- Score

3. How are corresponding different ecosystems used to gain an advantage in your organization?
<--- Score

4. How can asset inventory be tracked?

<--- Score

5. What role does Salesforce play in your ecosystem?
<--- Score

6. What does an external CPQ deployment look like to a buyer?
<--- Score

7. Why is it important to know the legend before the play begins?
<--- Score

8. Can the assistant send an active call directly to a manager?
<--- Score

9. Can work be performed on-site/off-site?
<--- Score

10. Are you able to apply a single due diligence framework to all your regulated products?
<--- Score

11. Can the system be accessed through the web?
<--- Score

12. What happens after the system is implemented and in operation?
<--- Score

13. How does the hardware environment influence the system architecture and its algorithms?
<--- Score

14. What is the added value for a Sales Rep?
<--- Score

15. How is the play unified in terms of time, space and character?
<--- Score

16. How does skills-based routing differ from queue-based routing?
<--- Score

17. What are the Salesforce IP Addresses & Domains to Whitelist?
<--- Score

18. Are you currently running the most recent version of your vendors software?
<--- Score

19. Where do you collect information about competing and complementary providers?
<--- Score

20. How do you get additional information?
<--- Score

21. How are customized reports generated?
<--- Score

22. What would be the value for quotation sentiment?
<--- Score

23. Which format currently will better facilitate access to electronic records through the use of assistive technologies?

<--- Score

24. Have any virtualization types been approved to be used?
<--- Score

25. How are different ecosystems used to gain an advantage in your organization?
<--- Score

26. Should you mobilize and socialize your CPQ?
<--- Score

27. Does it integrate with your existing applications?
<--- Score

28. How would you approach marketing to corresponding different areas of the world?
<--- Score

29. What might a configuration sound like?
<--- Score

30. What could shortening the sales cycle do for your business?
<--- Score

31. Why are you unable to view the resource hierarchy for your organization?
<--- Score

32. Have your rolled out CPQ globally?
<--- Score

33. Are you ready to take your small business to

new heights?
<--- Score

34. What is the sentiment on products compared to competitors in the web and on social media?
<--- Score

35. How robust is the contribution of morphological awareness to general spelling outcomes?
<--- Score

36. What is the calculated List Unit Price the user should see for Cloud Storage Support?
<--- Score

37. How will the provider follow-up on the order?
<--- Score

38. What are configuration attributes?
<--- Score

39. Can customers start a quote on one channel and finish it on another?
<--- Score

40. Where do you find the resources to test thoroughly?
<--- Score

41. Can assistant change or update the managers configuration?
<--- Score

42. Where are you in the market cycle?
<--- Score

43. How does skills-based routing work?
<--- Score

44. How does the system provide for fault tolerance?
<--- Score

45. What can an effective CPQ tool do?
<--- Score

46. What is/are the contract numbers for work?
<--- Score

47. Are you prepared for a new world of enterprise mobility?
<--- Score

48. What is so significant about the comprehensive systems and networking budget model?
<--- Score

49. Which deployment option is best for your sales team?
<--- Score

50. Where is your organization heading, what is the short term and long term strategy?
<--- Score

51. How are software ecosystems utilized in your organization?
<--- Score

52. Are your approval regulations increasing the length of the sales cycle?

<--- Score

53. How do you request admin assist?
<--- Score

54. Is the misallocation between monthly minimums and commodity rates the only thing you find troubling with staffs rate design?
<--- Score

55. Can it send customized alerts to sales, finance, legal, and other personnel?
<--- Score

56. What are other ways you could present the information or the skill?
<--- Score

57. Can implementing CPQ in your organization actually benefit your customers?
<--- Score

58. Should you adopt an alternative timeline for small requests, and, if so, how many poles should count as a small request and what deadlines should apply?
<--- Score

59. What is the order of execution when a new transaction is created?
<--- Score

60. Is your application multi or single-tenancy?
<--- Score

61. Where is the maximum or minimum value of a

quadratic equation located?
<--- Score

62. What is your user reconciliation policy?
<--- Score

63. Will the client like your artistic vision?
<--- Score

64. How do you empower your sales team to sell more effectively with less time?
<--- Score

65. Will you be employing contract workers for the work being completed?
<--- Score

66. Where would it be appropriate to add a blurb about quotation marks being used as a form of bias?
<--- Score

67. How often do you wear clothing with other organizations emblem?
<--- Score

68. Why should you teach vocabulary explicitly and systematically?
<--- Score

69. How similar is the project and the facility/location where it is being performed?
<--- Score

70. Is each staff member appraised on performance, at least annually?

<--- Score

71. Which combinations of options should you bundle?
<--- Score

72. How do you ensure that users embrace the new Salesforce?
<--- Score

73. What other products or services do you offer?
<--- Score

74. What application version is supported?
<--- Score

75. Do you see value gaps in your organization?
<--- Score

76. What connections did you make while reading?
<--- Score

77. Are guidelines necessary or helpful?
<--- Score

78. What is your channel strategy and structure, if any?
<--- Score

79. Are receipts deposited on a regular basis?
<--- Score

80. What is the role of reinforcement in early language acquisition?
<--- Score

81. How is that managed by your system?
<--- Score

82. Will tracking information be supplied on the purchase?
<--- Score

83. Are services compatible and complimentary?
<--- Score

84. Which type should be used for the product action?
<--- Score

85. How does more efficient quoting support your organizations business goals?
<--- Score

86. Will the system work smoothly and will users accept it?
<--- Score

87. Why is the contacts account information missing?
<--- Score

88. Is your business ready to move to the cloud?
<--- Score

89. What is your overall impression of other employees here?
<--- Score

90. Which option is the most appropriate for the CPQ Specialist to suggest first?
<--- Score

91. Who are your customers/Who do you help?
<--- Score

92. Where and who from do sales personnel get additional information?
<--- Score

93. Does the system provide alternate system wide conversations?
<--- Score

94. How often do you sell at full list price?
<--- Score

95. What happens when you delete a contact?
<--- Score

96. Why is it fair to test only whether prices are too low?
<--- Score

97. How do you quote service pricing on a product bundle?
<--- Score

98. Is there any charge for using local storage or a public cloud?
<--- Score

99. Which is an invalid Commerce rule type?
<--- Score

100. When creating a connection for a CPQ SOAP Endpoint in ICS, which format is expected?
<--- Score

101. Which code lists are supported for automatic configuration?
<--- Score

102. What is important to remember when setting a CPQ?
<--- Score

103. How does your organization respond?
<--- Score

104. What does your market place look like?
<--- Score

105. Do your systems tend to favour incumbents?
<--- Score

106. Is there an incumbent organization providing services today or in the recent past?
<--- Score

107. What are your discount schedules?
<--- Score

108. What additional services does your organization offer?
<--- Score

109. What activities interrupt selling time?
<--- Score

110. Who are the Independent Providers?
<--- Score

111. Do you always start your day with a specific

item, like a list or dashboard?
<--- Score

112. Do you assign multiple resource roles to a team member at the same time?
<--- Score

113. How would you approach marketing to different areas of the world?
<--- Score

114. Are services contradictory or redundant or excessive?
<--- Score

115. Does a quote involve the resources of more employees other than the sales rep?
<--- Score

116. How do successful organizations schedule project?
<--- Score

117. Are your end users experiencing bugs in production system?
<--- Score

118. How do you choose the right CPQ for your organization?
<--- Score

119. Can clients access a test/demo version of your service before making a purchase?
<--- Score

120. How can sales organizations create offers

faster, more accurate and more compelling?
<--- Score

121. Do you have either a trained spill response team or a contract with a spill response organization?
<--- Score

122. Where has the scheme/ project come from?
<--- Score

123. How are prospects converted from visitors?
<--- Score

124. What is the size limit of an array set in Configuration?
<--- Score

125. Are there any restrictions on use of funds on the systems change track?
<--- Score

126. Are you currently still undertaking any of activities?
<--- Score

127. How will you support your users after Go-Live?
<--- Score

128. Have you made any changes to the rate design from the rebuttal filing?
<--- Score

129. How do your employees get work done?
<--- Score

130. How do you update custom object records?
<--- Score

131. How receptive is the sales team to pricing guidance?
<--- Score

132. How do you provide more specific and informative feedback?
<--- Score

133. Does your organization experience channel conflict?
<--- Score

134. Does your organization have a system for the approval of log suppliers?
<--- Score

135. How do other organizations influence open source software communities?
<--- Score

136. Can system prompts be interrupted by experienced users?
<--- Score

137. How to handle dynamic change and capture management information?
<--- Score

138. What is the typical method of support for future software updates, and how are licensing upgrades handled?
<--- Score

139. How much selling power are you really getting from your sales teams?
<--- Score

140. When is the contract for the current vendor expiring?
<--- Score

141. Is organization sales strategy clearly stated?
<--- Score

142. How many support staff are located there?
<--- Score

143. Is pricing and product information from your erp always available to sales?
<--- Score

144. Is respondent capable of providing electronic invoicing through myfloridamarketplace?
<--- Score

145. What is the appropriate target for your organization?
<--- Score

146. Who can blame a sales rep for thinking a new sales tool like a CPQ will add more work?
<--- Score

147. Are time and attendance records kept for all employees by program, by funding source?
<--- Score

148. What are the options for promoting products

and services?
<--- Score

149. What is a recommended approach to keep in mind when implementing the Commerce pricing function?
<--- Score

150. What is the target date for contract execution?
<--- Score

151. Is there an incumbent/existing vendor providing services?
<--- Score

152. How do you manage the pace of your digital transformation projects?
<--- Score

153. Will the acquisition use a performance-based approach?
<--- Score

154. Which sources are used for finding out product and pricing information?
<--- Score

155. How is your sales organization currently structured?
<--- Score

156. Which hardware platforms does the system run on?
<--- Score

157. Is there leadership in price discovery among market makers?
<--- Score

158. Is mobile customer service right for you?
<--- Score

159. What limits your organizations innovation in Salesforce?
<--- Score

160. What are the market trends and industry profiles?
<--- Score

161. What are acceptable organization and product names?
<--- Score

162. Does the information match that set out in the guideline?
<--- Score

163. How many quotes do you generate in a year?
<--- Score

164. What are the most frequent technical approaches and associated products?
<--- Score

165. Are quoting errors common due to product that is unavailable, incorrectly priced, or out of date?
<--- Score

166. What is the average response time for a

typical inquiry?
<--- Score

167. Why is winning over senior management a best practice?
<--- Score

168. What is driving CPQ transformation?
<--- Score

169. What sound does ending start with?
<--- Score

170. Are you feeling the downward price pressure of an industry heading towards commoditization?
<--- Score

171. What partnerships do you have with technology vendors?
<--- Score

172. What currency is the quotation in?
<--- Score

173. Will the resources demanded by the method be worth it?
<--- Score

174. What are the values of the current quotation?
<--- Score

175. What in your mind triggers your responsibility independent of the entities that are pursuing own investigations?
<--- Score

176. Which partner functions are allowed for an item?
<--- Score

177. What type of support is offered?
<--- Score

178. Is there a beginning, middle, and end?
<--- Score

179. Which email integration product is right for your organization?
<--- Score

180. Does a suppliers business philosophy match that of the buying organization?
<--- Score

181. Are ineligible and incompatible products leading to order fallout and unhappy customers?
<--- Score

182. Who is responsible for your Salesforce instance?
<--- Score

183. Why should you test your alarm system and how often?
<--- Score

184. Is your organization publicly listed/traded?
<--- Score

185. How intuitive is your help information?
<--- Score

186. What are the most appropriate SaaS features for the suppliers offer to businesses?
<--- Score

187. How many users should be assigned?
<--- Score

188. How do you deliver with the same operation and equipment?
<--- Score

189. Which services are offered alongside the quoted technical packages?
<--- Score

190. How do you balance providing access versus providing quality with limited resources?
<--- Score

191. Which salesforce logos should be used?
<--- Score

192. Why must a billing platform enable recurring customer relationships?
<--- Score

193. Are you losing money due to errors during order creation in your erp?
<--- Score

194. How are contract changes managed and recorded?
<--- Score

195. What in your organizations view constitutes good trading experience?

<--- Score

196. Are your sales representatives frustrated with inaccurate product quotes and pricing?
<--- Score

197. How big is the visual & virtual CPQ market?
<--- Score

198. What was the highest year of organization you completed?
<--- Score

199. What would be the value for delivery time?
<--- Score

200. How do you educate new teams on your product mix, value and culture?
<--- Score

201. Is structure dependence an innate constraint?
<--- Score

202. How will staff attrition be managed?
<--- Score

203. Does service bundling reduce churn?
<--- Score

204. What are the negatives that come with joining ecosystems?
<--- Score

205. How do you associate one or more existing customer asset attributes with a specific condition?

<--- Score

206. Will the amended regulation help to ensure that all employees legal rights are respected?
<--- Score

207. Where do you get additional information on alt format?
<--- Score

208. Did you want the pricing quoted as fixed price or time and material?
<--- Score

209. Which conditional has the same truth value as its converse?
<--- Score

210. What import features are available for importing your business object?
<--- Score

211. Why is sales efficiency so important?
<--- Score

212. Why address the international side of business?
<--- Score

213. What are the different types of Salesforce partners?
<--- Score

214. Do you support configure, price, quote?
<--- Score

215. What performance indicators could be applied to project activities and outcomes?
<--- Score

216. How do other organizations expect to benefit from vendor experience?
<--- Score

217. How serious is your organization about sales transformation?
<--- Score

218. Are auto alerts available for extended time or for no action?
<--- Score

219. How do you take advantage of the dramatic growth in sales channels?
<--- Score

220. How do you perform tasks on behalf of another user?
<--- Score

221. What are the server types expected to be hosted?
<--- Score

222. What sales tools do your agents want?
<--- Score

223. What has been performance of markets in eliciting demand response?
<--- Score

224. Do you view a resource organization

hierarchy version as of a particular date?
<--- Score

225. How does cloud CPQ help provide error-free orders?
<--- Score

226. How are customers using your online self-services?
<--- Score

227. Is there a less burdensome method for addressing the purpose of the amended regulation?
<--- Score

228. What are the elements of a good practice service/support/policy/ approach?
<--- Score

229. What is your version of how to approach that?
<--- Score

230. When should businesses explore CPQ?
<--- Score

231. How is reporting configured, how are reports accessed?
<--- Score

232. What software is your organization currently using for quoting?
<--- Score

233. Are supervisory spot checks conducted on the quotations received?

<--- Score

234. Do you have custom markup in your head markup?
<--- Score

235. Is the sla included in the price quote?
<--- Score

236. What are the options for hosting the application?
<--- Score

237. Are you pointing in the wrong way?
<--- Score

238. Are you maximizing the sales potential of new digital markets?
<--- Score

239. Is valuable sales time being wasted on admin?
<--- Score

240. Do you really know what CPQ is all about?
<--- Score

241. How do you search and view resource information from other sources?
<--- Score

242. How will multiple submissions of the same resource be handled?
<--- Score

243. How do you ensure participation by all

relevant parties, including timely updates of information?
<--- Score

244. What do you do with Lightning components in flow screens?
<--- Score

245. How will your classification scheme to be maintained over time?
<--- Score

246. Which CPQ system is right for you?
<--- Score

247. Is the user to receive a periodic or daily notifications?
<--- Score

248. Does your system have an open reporting architecture?
<--- Score

249. What is the converse and the truth value of the converse conditional?
<--- Score

250. What type of encryption are you using?
<--- Score

251. How might thinking aloud before reading help your employees?
<--- Score

252. How are you helping each other win?
<--- Score

253. Do your customers purchase your products according to payment schedules?
<--- Score

254. Is value-based pricing always the best approach?
<--- Score

255. Are release dates and downtime slots negotiable?
<--- Score

256. What is the best way for you onboard your employees?
<--- Score

257. What are some reasons unemployment filings might have dropped, even while unemployment remains high?
<--- Score

258. Why should organizations implement changes early?
<--- Score

259. What type of customer segmentation are you using?
<--- Score

260. What do you want your internal communications strategy to do for your department?
<--- Score

261. Is a new rebrand happening after you

published your custom branded app?
<--- Score

262. Has any jurisdiction limited your practice in any way or by any other action?
<--- Score

263. Have you complied with all regulations relating to the operation of the collection of custom import duties?
<--- Score

264. What makes CPQ an imperative in the manufacturing industry?
<--- Score

265. Is your organization authorized to sell the products?
<--- Score

266. Is the default user interface consumer-grade?
<--- Score

267. When should you use trademark symbols in connection with Salesforce trademarks?
<--- Score

268. What do vendors in the market have to offer?
<--- Score

269. Will your organization commit to program implementation schedule?
<--- Score

270. Can the word cloud be used in naming?
<--- Score

271. Which configuration is valid for displaying the attributes?
<--- Score

272. What price-setting path is used by your organization?
<--- Score

273. What information would be most valuable if reflected in Salesforce?
<--- Score

274. How do corresponding pricing models compare?
<--- Score

275. Do you just make one point of clarification?
<--- Score

276. Does your organization have existing capacity to provide electronic and ecommerce ordering and billing?
<--- Score

277. Does system provide the ability to track time worked on tickets?
<--- Score

278. How do you provide incentives in a broad way for continuing efforts towards performance?
<--- Score

279. What is next for social marketing?
<--- Score

280. What is the correct Price Rule Setup?
<--- Score

281. Has the board experienced any significant changes to its operations?
<--- Score

282. How many times have people viewed and downloaded your file?
<--- Score

283. How does your organization show up?
<--- Score

284. What is configure, price, quote?
<--- Score

285. Does each market maker contribute equally to price discovery?
<--- Score

286. When can the reserve be accessed?
<--- Score

287. What is the correct way to refer to Salesforce?
<--- Score

288. Where are your CPQ support teams located?
<--- Score

289. Which inquiries, quotations, and orders are the basis for a particular delivery?
<--- Score

290. How many nights did you stay in organization?

<--- Score

291. How well did organization communicate important information to employees?
<--- Score

292. What benefits exactly can companies achieve through the use of CPQ?
<--- Score

293. Which rule is used to hide menu options in a single-select configurable attribute?
<--- Score

294. Should your organization provide encouragement for proprietary software vendors to support more open formats?
<--- Score

295. Do existing relationships between stakeholders contribute to a win-win strategy?
<--- Score

296. Have you ever been disciplined for an ethical violation by a professional association or organization?
<--- Score

297. Is vlan trunking supported or multiple vlans on a single interface?
<--- Score

298. How does your business create sales quotes?
<--- Score

299. How do you get new team members up to full

productivity faster?
<--- Score

300. How to submit when a CPQ is used?
<--- Score

301. What would be the value for payment terms template?
<--- Score

302. Which system is the source of truth?
<--- Score

303. Where do you find a CPQ system that can handle unlimited complexity?
<--- Score

304. Do you introduce promotions or update pricing easily to your sales teams?
<--- Score

305. Is it responsible for your salesforce instance?
<--- Score

306. How is record type access specified?
<--- Score

307. How do you interpret functions that arise in applications in terms of context?
<--- Score

308. What type of health insurance do you have?
<--- Score

309. What is the maximum number of simultaneous calls that can be handled by the PC-

based attendant console application?
<--- Score

310. Can the network automatically detect the presence of the IP phones?
<--- Score

311. What good is the best functionality if only a select few in your organization can access it?
<--- Score

312. How are you keeping in touch with your customer?
<--- Score

313. How do you know when the order was placed/ booked/delivered?
<--- Score

314. What is the difference in employee organizational commitment between Cornerstone and non-Cornerstone sophomore employees?
<--- Score

315. How are sales leaders to succeed in an environment?
<--- Score

316. What are the best predictors of employee organizational commitment?
<--- Score

317. Which representatives close the most business?
<--- Score

318. How do you align your people with the goal of achieving more favorable prices?
<--- Score

319. Will your organization consider modification of the pricing model to market competitive rates structures?
<--- Score

320. How much did pain interfere with your usual activities?
<--- Score

321. What if there is a change in the rate of pay?
<--- Score

322. Have multiple products, with multiple pricing tiers, and multiple concurrent discounts?
<--- Score

323. How can employees help employees deal constructively with conflict?
<--- Score

324. Are tamper-resistant/abuse-deterrent formulation less attractive in the illicit market?
<--- Score

325. What other resources are available?
<--- Score

326. Do employees with and without lexical retrieval weaknesses respond differently to instruction?
<--- Score

327. Why is pricing technology of interest?
<--- Score

328. Will you have the ability to exclude others?
<--- Score

329. Which access type is assigned to a user of a partner organization when it is created?
<--- Score

330. What is the total balance in all your joint accounts?
<--- Score

331. Where do you send your application?
<--- Score

332. What about situations where your organization is managing non customer relationships?
<--- Score

333. What gaps exist in your organizations intellectual property portfolio?
<--- Score

334. Are quotations sought for amounts greater than agreed levels?
<--- Score

335. How much time is between product configuration and order?
<--- Score

336. How do you place an economic value on insight?

<--- Score

337. How concerned about your intellectual growth are your organization here?
<--- Score

338. What is the estimated time that participants spend on your project?
<--- Score

339. What are the hottest areas for SaaS apps?
<--- Score

340. Are cash receipts from accounts receivable or other sources mixed with petty cash funds?
<--- Score

341. Will your organizations of the stream be altered or modified?
<--- Score

342. Does it include a modeling interface?
<--- Score

343. How much time will the interviews and selection take?
<--- Score

344. How should the CPQ Admin configure the bundle?
<--- Score

345. What account records do the different record sets permit you to search?
<--- Score

346. How do you empower your channel sales teams to succeed in practicing core competencies?
<--- Score

347. Are you utilizing the versioning features available in your source code repository?
<--- Score

348. Do the objectives at each level contribute to the achievement of objectives at the next higher level?
<--- Score

349. What is the point of the stacks approach?
<--- Score

350. How is vertical integration of tools enabled?
<--- Score

351. What contact records do the different records sets permit you to search?
<--- Score

352. What vendor do you currently rely on for your configure-price-quote system?
<--- Score

353. Is your organization ready for one-to-one marketing?
<--- Score

354. How should your organization address the long term preservation of its electronic records?
<--- Score

355. Does client have a history of mental health

services?
<--- Score

356. Are marketing activities appropriate to the project?
<--- Score

357. Should bigmachines customers continue to call bigmachines for customers support?
<--- Score

358. How do you track customer-facing activities?
<--- Score

359. What customer/product/deal attributes correlate with wins?
<--- Score

360. What is the highest number of IP devices currently supported under a single instance of the software?
<--- Score

361. Can you do all this work?
<--- Score

362. How much is that worth to your organization over the next year?
<--- Score

363. Do you get angry and aggressive when embarrassed or frustrated?
<--- Score

364. How did the order of the quotations affect your interest in the story?

<--- Score

365. Is the respondent on the suspended vendor list or have any open complaints to vendor?
<--- Score

366. What is your organization model?
<--- Score

367. Do existing stakeholders contribute to a win-win strategy?
<--- Score

368. How do you find and hire great sales and marketing talent?
<--- Score

369. What happens when the user specifies a new seed?
<--- Score

370. Does the complexity of product configurations affect your margins?
<--- Score

371. What is your overall impression of the other employees here?
<--- Score

372. What resources are available to you?
<--- Score

373. Does the structure remain appropriate to the business?
<--- Score

374. What if customers want to prepay subscription up front versus being billed each month?
<--- Score

375. What is the critical information?
<--- Score

376. When you do quote, why would the quote be a credible signal to the market?
<--- Score

377. How can service cloud help your organization?
<--- Score

378. What is your organization Procedure?
<--- Score

379. What benefits does the CPQ offer?
<--- Score

380. What is the technical knowledge and/or expertise of the supplier?
<--- Score

381. Will sales and back-office be ready on day one?
<--- Score

382. Why is the term marketing surrounded by confusion?
<--- Score

383. What should be done so that the pricing is rounded to the expected value?

<--- Score

384. Do existing objectives contribute to a win-win strategy?
<--- Score

385. What is your timeline for implementation and/or launch?
<--- Score

386. Are there any incentive property management fees?
<--- Score

387. What type of non-cash benefits did you receive in the last financial year?
<--- Score

388. Are financial reports prepared monthly for internal management for internal management purposes?
<--- Score

389. What does a CPQ deployment look like from the buyers perspective?
<--- Score

390. Are you allowed to request a higher goal for your specific project/organization?
<--- Score

391. Will there be a request for information, which subjects might consider to be personal or sensitive?
<--- Score

Add up total points for this section:
_____ = Total points for this section

Divided by: ______ (number of statements answered) = ______ Average score for this section

Transfer your score to the Salesforce CPQ Index at the beginning of the Self-Assessment.

Salesforce CPQ and Managing Projects, Criteria for Project Managers:

1.0 Initiating Process Group: Salesforce CPQ

1. Information sharing?

2. Were sponsors and decision makers available when needed outside regularly scheduled meetings?

3. What do they need to know about the Salesforce CPQ project?

4. Who is involved in each phase?

5. What are the overarching issues of your organization?

6. Do you understand the quality and control criteria that must be achieved for successful Salesforce CPQ project completion?

7. In which Salesforce CPQ project management process group is the detailed Salesforce CPQ project budget created?

8. Are the Salesforce CPQ project team and stakeholders meeting regularly and using a meeting agenda and taking notes to accurately document what is being covered and what happened in the weekly meetings?

9. What were things that you need to improve?

10. How will it affect me?

11. What are the tools and techniques to be used in

each phase?

12. How will you know you did it?

13. Which six sigma dmaic phase focuses on why and how defects and errors occur?

14. Did the Salesforce CPQ project team have the right skills?

15. How well did you do?

16. During which stage of Risk planning are risks prioritized based on probability and impact?

17. How will you do it?

18. What were things that you did very well and want to do the same again on the next Salesforce CPQ project?

19. Are identified risks being monitored properly, are new risks arising during the Salesforce CPQ project or are foreseen risks occurring?

20. If the risk event occurs, what will you do?

1.1 Project Charter: Salesforce CPQ

21. Customer: who are you doing the Salesforce CPQ project for?

22. Are you building in-house ?

23. How will you know a change is an improvement?

24. Who is the Salesforce CPQ project Manager?

25. What is the purpose of the Salesforce CPQ project?

26. Who is the sponsor?

27. Run it as as a startup?

28. If finished, on what date did it finish?

29. Are there special technology requirements?

30. Environmental stewardship and sustainability considerations: what is the process that will be used to ensure compliance with the environmental stewardship policy?

31. Who are the stakeholders?

32. Why do you need to manage scope?

33. Is it an improvement over existing products?

34. When do you use a Salesforce CPQ project Charter?

35. What changes can you make to improve?

36. How are Salesforce CPQ projects different from operations?

37. Will this replace an existing product?

38. Assumptions and constraints: what assumptions were made in defining the Salesforce CPQ project?

39. Salesforce CPQ project background: what is the primary motivation for this Salesforce CPQ project?

40. What ideas do you have for initial tests of change (PDSA cycles)?

1.2 Stakeholder Register: Salesforce CPQ

41. What is the power of the stakeholder?

42. How big is the gap?

43. Who is managing stakeholder engagement?

44. Who wants to talk about Security?

45. What are the major Salesforce CPQ project milestones requiring communications or providing communications opportunities?

46. How should employers make voices heard?

47. How will reports be created?

48. What opportunities exist to provide communications?

49. Is your organization ready for change?

50. What & Why?

51. How much influence do they have on the Salesforce CPQ project?

1.3 Stakeholder Analysis Matrix: Salesforce CPQ

52. Will the impacts be local, national or international?

53. Vulnerable groups; who are the vulnerable groups that might be affected by the Salesforce CPQ project?

54. Which conditions out of the control of the management are crucial for the achievement of the immediate objective?

55. Who is directly responsible for decisions on issues important to the Salesforce CPQ project?

56. Alliances: with which other actors is the actor allied, how are they interconnected?

57. Do the stakeholders goals and expectations support or conflict with the Salesforce CPQ project goals?

58. Price, value, quality?

59. Who will be responsible for managing the outcome?

60. Processes, systems, it, communications?

61. Advantages of proposition?

62. What is the stakeholders name, what is function?

63. Vital contracts and partners?

64. How does the Salesforce CPQ project involve consultations or collaboration with other organizations?

65. Which resources are required?

66. Competitive advantages?

67. What can the Salesforce CPQ projects outcome be used for?

68. Sustainable financial backing?

69. Reliability of data, plan predictability?

70. Sustaining internal capabilities?

71. Would it be fair to say that cost is a controlling criteria?

2.0 Planning Process Group: Salesforce CPQ

72. The Salesforce CPQ project charter is created in which Salesforce CPQ project management process group?

73. How are it Salesforce CPQ projects different?

74. How well did the chosen processes fit the needs of the Salesforce CPQ project?

75. How well will the chosen processes produce the expected results?

76. Will the products created live up to the necessary quality?

77. Is your organization showing technical capacity and leadership commitment to keep working with the Salesforce CPQ project and to repeat it?

78. Contingency planning. if a risk event occurs, what will you do?

79. Is the identification of the problems, inequalities and gaps, with respective causes, clear in the Salesforce CPQ project?

80. How well defined and documented are the Salesforce CPQ project management processes you chose to use?

81. Why is it important to determine activity sequencing on Salesforce CPQ projects?

82. Salesforce CPQ project assessment; why did you do this Salesforce CPQ project?

83. When will the Salesforce CPQ project be done?

84. Is the duration of the program sufficient to ensure a cycle that will Salesforce CPQ project the sustainability of the interventions?

85. What business situation is being addressed?

86. What factors are contributing to progress or delay in the achievement of products and results?

87. If a task is partitionable, is this a sufficient condition to reduce the Salesforce CPQ project duration?

88. To what extent have public/private national resources and/or counterparts been mobilized to contribute to the programs objective and produce results and impacts?

89. In what way has the program contributed towards the issue culture and development included on the public agenda?

90. You did your readings, yes?

91. Just how important is your work to the overall success of the Salesforce CPQ project?

2.1 Project Management Plan: Salesforce CPQ

92. What does management expect of PMs?

93. Is there an incremental analysis/cost effectiveness analysis of proposed mitigation features based on an approved method and using an accepted model?

94. What are the assigned resources?

95. What would you do differently?

96. What are the assumptions?

97. Was the peer (technical) review of the cost estimates duly coordinated with the cost estimate center of expertise and addressed in the review documentation and certification?

98. Will you add a schedule and diagram?

99. Do the proposed changes from the Salesforce CPQ project include any significant risks to safety?

100. Are there non-structural buyout or relocation recommendations?

101. Development trends and opportunities. What if the positive direction and vision of your organization causes expected trends to change?

102. If the Salesforce CPQ project is complex or

scope is specialized, do you have appropriate and/or qualified staff available to perform the tasks?

103. Are there any scope changes proposed for a previously authorized Salesforce CPQ project?

104. Is mitigation authorized or recommended?

105. What happened during the process that you found interesting?

106. What are the constraints?

107. Do there need to be organizational changes?

108. If the Salesforce CPQ project management plan is a comprehensive document that guides you in Salesforce CPQ project execution and control, then what should it NOT contain?

109. Who manages integration?

110. Why Change?

2.2 Scope Management Plan: Salesforce CPQ

111. When is corrective or preventative action required?

112. Is current scope of the Salesforce CPQ project substantially different than that originally defined?

113. Pop quiz – which are the same inputs as in scope planning?

114. Is it standard practice to formally commit stakeholders to the Salesforce CPQ project via agreements?

115. Is the steering committee active in Salesforce CPQ project oversight?

116. Does the business case include how the Salesforce CPQ project aligns with your organizations strategic goals & objectives?

117. Time estimation – how much time will be needed?

118. Has the selected plan been formulated using cost effectiveness and incremental analysis techniques?

119. Is stakeholder involvement adequate?

120. Are alternatives safe, functional, constructible, economical, reasonable and sustainable?

121. Has your organization readiness assessment been conducted?

122. Are there any windfall benefits that would accrue to the Salesforce CPQ project sponsor or other parties?

123. Are written status reports provided on a designated frequent basis?

124. Is there an on-going process in place to monitor Salesforce CPQ project risks?

125. How do you know when you are finished?

126. Are stakeholders aware and supportive of the principles and practices of modern software estimation?

127. Pop quiz – what changed on Salesforce CPQ project scope statement input?

128. For which criterion is it tolerable not to meet the original parameters?

129. Does the Salesforce CPQ project team have the skills necessary to successfully complete current Salesforce CPQ project(s) and support the application?

130. Are any non-compliance issues that exist due to organizations practices?

2.3 Requirements Management Plan: Salesforce CPQ

131. How will requirements be managed?

132. Do you have an agreed upon process for alerting the Salesforce CPQ project Manager if a request for change in requirements leads to a product scope change?

133. Is requirements work dependent on any other specific Salesforce CPQ project or non-Salesforce CPQ project activities (e.g. funding, approvals, procurement)?

134. Who will do the reporting and to whom will reports be delivered?

135. What is the earliest finish date for this Salesforce CPQ project if it is scheduled to start on ...?

136. Who came up with this requirement?

137. Did you distinguish the scope of work the contractor(s) will be required to do?

138. Define the help desk model. who will take full responsibility?

139. Do you understand the role that each stakeholder will play in the requirements process?

140. How detailed should the Salesforce CPQ project

get?

141. Did you provide clear and concise specifications?

142. Did you get proper approvals?

143. Controlling Salesforce CPQ project requirements involves monitoring the status of the Salesforce CPQ project requirements and managing changes to the requirements. Who is responsible for monitoring and tracking the Salesforce CPQ project requirements?

144. Why manage requirements?

145. Do you expect stakeholders to be cooperative?

146. Are all the stakeholders ready for the transition into the user community?

147. How will the requirements become prioritized?

148. Will the Salesforce CPQ project requirements become approved in writing?

149. Is the user satisfied?

150. Who will initially review the Salesforce CPQ project work or products to ensure it meets the applicable acceptance criteria?

2.4 Requirements Documentation: Salesforce CPQ

151. Are there legal issues?

152. How much testing do you need to do to prove that your system is safe?

153. What kind of entity is a problem ?

154. What are the acceptance criteria?

155. What images does it conjure?

156. What are current process problems?

157. Can the requirement be changed without a large impact on other requirements?

158. How linear / iterative is your Requirements Gathering process (or will it be)?

159. Are there any requirements conflicts?

160. How do you get the user to tell you what they want?

161. How does the proposed Salesforce CPQ project contribute to the overall objectives of your organization?

162. Consistency. are there any requirements conflicts?

163. Are all functions required by the customer included?

164. Who is involved?

165. What will be the integration problems?

166. How to document system requirements?

167. What variations exist for a process?

168. Where are business rules being captured?

169. Is new technology needed?

170. What happens when requirements are wrong?

2.5 Requirements Traceability Matrix: Salesforce CPQ

171. How will it affect the stakeholders personally in career?

172. What is the WBS?

173. How do you manage scope?

174. Will you use a Requirements Traceability Matrix?

175. Describe the process for approving requirements so they can be added to the traceability matrix and Salesforce CPQ project work can be performed. Will the Salesforce CPQ project requirements become approved in writing?

176. Is there a requirements traceability process in place?

177. What are the chronologies, contingencies, consequences, criteria?

178. Why use a WBS?

179. Do you have a clear understanding of all subcontracts in place?

180. Why do you manage scope?

181. What percentage of Salesforce CPQ projects are producing traceability matrices between

requirements and other work products?

182. How small is small enough?

2.6 Project Scope Statement: Salesforce CPQ

183. Is the plan for your organization of the Salesforce CPQ project resources adequate?

184. Are there adequate Salesforce CPQ project control systems?

185. Has the Salesforce CPQ project scope statement been reviewed as part of the baseline process?

186. Is the quality function identified and assigned?

187. Will statistics related to QA be collected, trends analyzed, and problems raised as issues?

188. Who will you recommend approve the change, and when do you recommend the change reviews occur?

189. Salesforce CPQ project lead, team lead, solution architect?

190. Will there be a Change Control Process in place?

191. Were potential customers involved early in the planning process?

192. Are the meetings set up to have assigned note takers that will add action/issues to the issue list?

193. Is there a Change Management Board?

194. Write a brief purpose statement for this Salesforce CPQ project. Include a business justification statement. What is the product of this Salesforce CPQ project?

195. Is an issue management process documented and filed?

196. Is the Salesforce CPQ project sponsor function identified and defined?

197. Risks?

198. What should you drop in order to add something new?

199. What are the defined meeting materials?

200. Elements of scope management that deal with concept development ?

201. What is the most common tool for helping define the detail?

2.7 Assumption and Constraint Log: Salesforce CPQ

202. How can you prevent/fix violations?

203. Is the steering committee active in Salesforce CPQ project oversight?

204. Model-building: what data-analytic strategies are useful when building proportional-hazards models?

205. Is staff trained on the software technologies that are being used on the Salesforce CPQ project?

206. What do you log?

207. Are there ways to reduce the time it takes to get something approved?

208. Does the Salesforce CPQ project have a formal Salesforce CPQ project Plan?

209. Are formal code reviews conducted?

210. Diagrams and tables are included to account for complex concepts and increase overall readability?

211. Are funding and staffing resource estimates sufficiently detailed and documented for use in planning and tracking the Salesforce CPQ project?

212. Can the requirements be traced to the appropriate components of the solution, as well as

test scripts?

213. What weaknesses do you have?

214. Does the document/deliverable meet all requirements (for example, statement of work) specific to this deliverable?

215. Are there processes defining how software will be developed including development methods, overall timeline for development, software product standards, and traceability?

216. Has a Salesforce CPQ project Communications Plan been developed?

217. Have Salesforce CPQ project management standards and procedures been established and documented?

218. If it is out of compliance, should the process be amended or should the Plan be amended?

219. Are there nonconformance issues?

220. What worked well?

221. What would you gain if you spent time working to improve this process?

2.8 Work Breakdown Structure: Salesforce CPQ

222. How many levels?

223. Why would you develop a Work Breakdown Structure?

224. When does it have to be done?

225. What is the probability of completing the Salesforce CPQ project in less that xx days?

226. What is the probability that the Salesforce CPQ project duration will exceed xx weeks?

227. Can you make it?

228. Is the work breakdown structure (wbs) defined and is the scope of the Salesforce CPQ project clear with assigned deliverable owners?

229. How far down?

230. Is it still viable?

231. When do you stop?

232. Why is it useful?

233. Who has to do it?

234. Where does it take place?

235. How big is a work-package?

236. What has to be done?

237. Do you need another level?

2.9 WBS Dictionary: Salesforce CPQ

238. Where engineering standards or other internal work measurement systems are used, is there a formal relationship between corresponding values and work package budgets?

239. Are the variances between budgeted and actual indirect costs identified and analyzed at the level of assigned responsibility for control (indirect pool, department, etc.)?

240. Are data elements (BCWS, BCWP, and ACWP) progressively summarized from the detail level to the contract level through the CWBS?

241. Is data disseminated to the contractors management timely, accurate, and usable?

242. Are overhead budgets and costs being handled according to the disclosure statement when applicable, or otherwise properly classified (for example, engineering overhead, IR&D)?

243. Contemplated overhead expenditure for each period based on the best information currently available?

244. Changes in the nature of the overhead requirements?

245. What is the end result of a work package?

246. Performance to date and material commitment?

247. Does the contractor use objective results, design reviews and tests to trace schedule performance?

248. Are budgets or values assigned to work packages and planning packages in terms of dollars, hours, or other measurable units?

249. Are control accounts opened and closed based on the start and completion of work contained therein?

250. Are the requirements for all items of overhead established by rational, traceable processes?

251. Does the sum of all work package budgets plus planning packages within control accounts equal the budgets assigned to the already stated control accounts?

252. Are detailed work packages planned as far in advance as practicable?

253. Is future work which cannot be planned in detail subdivided to the extent practicable for budgeting and scheduling purposes?

254. Does the contractors system provide for determination of price variance by comparing planned Vs actual commitments?

255. Are procedures in existence that control replanning of unopened work packages, and are corresponding procedures adhered to?

256. Is work properly classified as measured effort,

LOE, or apportioned effort and appropriately separated?

2.10 Schedule Management Plan: Salesforce CPQ

257. Is there anything planned that does not need to be here?

258. What happens if a warning is triggered?

259. Is there a requirements change management processes in place?

260. Does the schedule have reasonable float?

261. Are all attributes of the activities defined, including risk and uncertainty?

262. Are all vendor contracts closed out?

263. Are Salesforce CPQ project contact logs kept up to date?

264. Is current scope of the Salesforce CPQ project substantially different than that originally defined?

265. Are all activities captured and do they address all approved work scope in the Salesforce CPQ project baseline?

266. Are the activity durations realistic and at an appropriate level of detail for effective management?

267. Are Salesforce CPQ project leaders committed to this Salesforce CPQ project full time?

268. Staffing Requirements?

269. Are the results of quality assurance reviews provided to affected groups & individuals?

270. Why time management?

271. Are adequate resources provided for the quality assurance function?

272. Is the quality assurance team identified?

273. Are Salesforce CPQ project team members committed fulltime?

274. Has a structured approach been used to break work effort into manageable components (WBS)?

275. Is there an approved case?

276. Why conduct schedule analysis?

2.11 Activity List: Salesforce CPQ

277. How difficult will it be to do specific activities on this Salesforce CPQ project?

278. What is the total time required to complete the Salesforce CPQ project if no delays occur?

279. What went well?

280. Can you determine the activity that must finish, before this activity can start?

281. When do the individual activities need to start and finish?

282. For other activities, how much delay can be tolerated?

283. What is the LF and LS for each activity?

284. What did not go as well?

285. How detailed should a Salesforce CPQ project get?

286. How should ongoing costs be monitored to try to keep the Salesforce CPQ project within budget?

287. How can the Salesforce CPQ project be displayed graphically to better visualize the activities?

288. The wbs is developed as part of a joint planning session. and how do you know that youhave done this

right?

289. What are you counting on?

290. What are the critical bottleneck activities?

291. What is the probability the Salesforce CPQ project can be completed in xx weeks?

292. Should you include sub-activities?

293. How will it be performed?

294. How much slack is available in the Salesforce CPQ project?

295. What is your organizations history in doing similar activities?

2.12 Activity Attributes: Salesforce CPQ

296. How else could the items be grouped?

297. Do you feel very comfortable with your prediction?

298. Time for overtime?

299. Resources to accomplish the work?

300. What conclusions/generalizations can you draw from this?

301. Have you identified the Activity Leveling Priority code value on each activity?

302. Can more resources be added?

303. Have constraints been applied to the start and finish milestones for the phases?

304. Were there other ways you could have organized the data to achieve similar results?

305. What activity do you think you should spend the most time on?

306. Where else does it apply?

307. Activity: what is In the Bag?

308. Does your organization of the data change its meaning?

309. Is there a trend during the year?

310. What is the general pattern here?

311. How many resources do you need to complete the work scope within a limit of X number of days?

312. What went wrong?

313. Which method produces the more accurate cost assignment?

2.13 Milestone List: Salesforce CPQ

314. Political effects?

315. How late can each activity be finished and started?

316. It is to be a narrative text providing the crucial aspects of your Salesforce CPQ project proposal answering what, who, how, when and where?

317. Gaps in capabilities?

318. How soon can the activity start?

319. Insurmountable weaknesses?

320. What specific improvements did you make to the Salesforce CPQ project proposal since the previous time?

321. Do you foresee any technical risks or developmental challenges?

322. Timescales, deadlines and pressures?

323. Milestone pages should display the UserID of the person who added the milestone. Does a report or query exist that provides this audit information?

324. Identify critical paths (one or more) and which activities are on the critical path?

325. What would happen if a delivery of material was

one week late?

326. How will the milestone be verified?

327. Which path is the critical path?

328. Information and research?

2.14 Network Diagram: Salesforce CPQ

329. What is the completion time?

330. Which type of network diagram allows you to depict four types of dependencies?

331. What activities must occur simultaneously with this activity?

332. What are the tools?

333. What job or jobs precede it?

334. What activity must be completed immediately before this activity can start?

335. Why must you schedule milestones, such as reviews, throughout the Salesforce CPQ project?

336. If a current contract exists, can you provide the vendor name, contract start, and contract expiration date?

337. What controls the start and finish of a job?

338. What to do and When?

339. Review the logical flow of the network diagram. Take a look at which activities you have first and then sequence the activities. Do they make sense?

340. If x is long, what would be the completion time if you break x into two parallel parts of y weeks and z weeks?

341. What activities must follow this activity?

342. What is the lowest cost to complete this Salesforce CPQ project in xx weeks?

343. What are the Key Success Factors?

344. What is the probability of completing the Salesforce CPQ project in less that xx days?

345. What job or jobs could run concurrently?

346. How confident can you be in your milestone dates and the delivery date?

347. What must be completed before an activity can be started?

348. Where do you schedule uncertainty time?

2.15 Activity Resource Requirements: Salesforce CPQ

349. How do you manage time?

350. How many signatures do you require on a check and does this match what is in your policy and procedures?

351. What is the Work Plan Standard?

352. Which logical relationship does the PDM use most often?

353. How do you handle petty cash?

354. Anything else?

355. Organizational Applicability?

356. When does monitoring begin?

357. Other support in specific areas?

358. Do you use tools like decomposition and rolling-wave planning to produce the activity list and other outputs?

359. Are there unresolved issues that need to be addressed?

360. What are constraints that you might find during the Human Resource Planning process?

361. Why do you do that?

2.16 Resource Breakdown Structure: Salesforce CPQ

362. Who will be used as a Salesforce CPQ project team member?

363. What is the primary purpose of the human resource plan?

364. Changes based on input from stakeholders?

365. Are the required resources available?

366. Who is allowed to perform which functions?

367. Any changes from stakeholders?

368. Why do you do it?

369. Who needs what information?

370. What went right?

371. What are the requirements for resource data?

372. What defines a successful Salesforce CPQ project?

373. Why is this important?

374. What is the difference between % Complete and % work?

375. How should the information be delivered?

376. What is Salesforce CPQ project communication management?

377. Which resources should be in the resource pool?

378. What is the purpose of assigning and documenting responsibility?

2.17 Activity Duration Estimates: Salesforce CPQ

379. If the optimiztic estimate for an activity is 12days, and the pessimistic estimate is 18days, what is the standard deviation of this activity?

380. What do you think about the WBSs for them?

381. What is the difference between using brainstorming and the Delphi technique for risk identification?

382. What is the BEST thing for the Salesforce CPQ project manager to do?

383. What questions do you have about the sample documents provided?

384. How does a Salesforce CPQ project life cycle differ from a product life cycle?

385. Who has the PRIMARY responsibility to solve this problem?

386. Is the cost performance monitored to identify variances from the plan?

387. Account for the four frames of organizations. How can they help Salesforce CPQ project managers understand your organizational context for Salesforce CPQ projects?

388. How is the Salesforce CPQ project doing?

389. Describe Salesforce CPQ project integration management in your own words. How does Salesforce CPQ project integration management relate to the Salesforce CPQ project life cycle, stakeholders, and the other Salesforce CPQ project management knowledge areas?

390. Does a process exist to determine which risk events to accept and which events to disregard?

391. Who will be the main sponsor for it?

392. Are procedures documented for managing risks?

393. How have experts such as Deming, Juran, Crosby, and Taguchi affected the quality movement and todays use of Six Sigma?

394. Do you think Salesforce CPQ project managers of large information technology Salesforce CPQ projects need strong technical skills?

395. Do they make sense?

2.18 Duration Estimating Worksheet: Salesforce CPQ

396. Why estimate time and cost?

397. How should ongoing costs be monitored to try to keep the Salesforce CPQ project within budget?

398. What is an Average Salesforce CPQ project?

399. What questions do you have?

400. What is your role?

401. What is cost and Salesforce CPQ project cost management?

402. Is the Salesforce CPQ project responsive to community need?

403. Small or large Salesforce CPQ project?

404. What info is needed?

405. When does your organization expect to be able to complete it?

406. Can the Salesforce CPQ project be constructed as planned?

407. What utility impacts are there?

408. What is next?

409. Science = process: remember the scientific method?

410. When, then?

411. Does the Salesforce CPQ project provide innovative ways for stakeholders to overcome obstacles or deliver better outcomes?

412. Is this operation cost effective?

2.19 Project Schedule: Salesforce CPQ

413. To what degree is do you feel the entire team was committed to the Salesforce CPQ project schedule?

414. Activity charts and bar charts are graphical representations of a Salesforce CPQ project schedule ...how do they differ?

415. Salesforce CPQ project work estimates Who is managing the work estimate quality of work tasks in the Salesforce CPQ project schedule?

416. How much slack is available in the Salesforce CPQ project?

417. Is the Salesforce CPQ project schedule available for all Salesforce CPQ project team members to review?

418. Are the original Salesforce CPQ project schedule and budget realistic?

419. Verify that the update is accurate. Are all remaining durations correct?

420. It allows the Salesforce CPQ project to be delivered on schedule. How Do you Use Schedules?

421. How can slack be negative?

422. How do you manage Salesforce CPQ project Risk?

423. Are procedures defined by which the Salesforce

CPQ project schedule may be changed?

424. Understand the constraints used in preparing the schedule. Are activities connected because logic dictates the order in which others occur?

425. If there are any qualifying green components to this Salesforce CPQ project, what portion of the total Salesforce CPQ project cost is green?

426. Are activities connected because logic dictates the order in which others occur?

427. Why or why not?

428. Month Salesforce CPQ project take?

429. How do you use schedules?

430. Your Salesforce CPQ project management plan results in a Salesforce CPQ project schedule that is too long. If the Salesforce CPQ project network diagram cannot change and you have extra personnel resources, what is the BEST thing to do?

431. How can you address that situation?

2.20 Cost Management Plan: Salesforce CPQ

432. Does the business case include how the Salesforce CPQ project aligns with your organizations strategic goals & objectives?

433. Is it standard practice to formally commit stakeholders to the Salesforce CPQ project via agreements?

434. Milestones – what are the key dates in executing the contract plan?

435. Is the schedule updated on a periodic basis?

436. Are tasks tracked by hours?

437. Were Salesforce CPQ project team members involved in detailed estimating and scheduling?

438. Does the Salesforce CPQ project have a Quality Culture?

439. What are the Salesforce CPQ project objectives?

440. Best practices implementation – How will change management be applied to this Salesforce CPQ project?

441. Are actuals compared against estimates to analyze and correct variances?

442. Risk Analysis?

443. What will be the split of responsibilities of progress measurement and controls among the owner, contractor, subcontractors, and vendors?

444. How relevant is this attribute to this Salesforce CPQ project or audit?

445. Are Salesforce CPQ project contact logs kept up to date?

446. Change types and category – What are the types of changes and what are the techniques to report and control changes?

447. Are vendor invoices audited for accuracy before payment?

448. What would you do differently what did not work?

449. Are meeting minutes captured and sent out after the meeting?

450. What threats might prevent you from getting there?

2.21 Activity Cost Estimates: Salesforce CPQ

451. Does the activity rely on a common set of tools to carry it out?

452. Does the activity use a common approach or business function to deliver its results?

453. Can you change your activities?

454. What makes a good expected result statement?

455. What is the estimators estimating history?

456. What is the activity recast of the budget?

457. How quickly can the task be done with the skills available?

458. How many activities should you have?

459. What were things that you did very well and want to do the same again on the next Salesforce CPQ project?

460. Measurable - are the targets measurable?

461. What skill level is required to do the job?

462. Does the estimator estimate by task or by person?

463. How do you allocate indirect costs to activities?

464. What are the audit requirements?

465. Padding is bad and contingencies are good. what is the difference?

466. Was the consultant knowledgeable about the program?

467. Vac -variance at completion, how much over/ under budget do you expect to be?

2.22 Cost Estimating Worksheet: Salesforce CPQ

468. Can a trend be established from historical performance data on the selected measure and are the criteria for using trend analysis or forecasting methods met?

469. What can be included?

470. Who is best positioned to know and assist in identifying corresponding factors?

471. What will others want?

472. How will the results be shared and to whom?

473. Does the Salesforce CPQ project provide innovative ways for stakeholders to overcome obstacles or deliver better outcomes?

474. Value pocket identification & quantification what are value pockets?

475. Will the Salesforce CPQ project collaborate with the local community and leverage resources?

476. What additional Salesforce CPQ project(s) could be initiated as a result of this Salesforce CPQ project?

477. Ask: are others positioned to know, are others credible, and will others cooperate?

478. What is the purpose of estimating?

479. Is the Salesforce CPQ project responsive to community need?

480. What happens to any remaining funds not used?

481. What costs are to be estimated?

482. Is it feasible to establish a control group arrangement?

483. Identify the timeframe necessary to monitor progress and collect data to determine how the selected measure has changed?

484. What is the estimated labor cost today based upon this information?

2.23 Cost Baseline: Salesforce CPQ

485. What is cost and Salesforce CPQ project cost management?

486. Does the suggested change request seem to represent a necessary enhancement to the product?

487. Verify business objectives. Are others appropriate, and well-articulated?

488. Are you asking management for something as a result of this update?

489. Salesforce CPQ project goals -should others be reconsidered?

490. Does a process exist for establishing a cost baseline to measure Salesforce CPQ project performance?

491. What do you want to measure ?

492. Has the Salesforce CPQ project (or Salesforce CPQ project phase) been evaluated against each objective established in the product description and Integrated Salesforce CPQ project Plan?

493. What is the reality?

494. Has the Salesforce CPQ projected annual cost to operate and maintain the product(s) or service(s) been approved and funded?

495. Pcs for your new business. what would the life cycle costs be?

496. Does the suggested change request represent a desired enhancement to the products functionality?

497. How long are you willing to wait before you find out were late?

498. Where do changes come from?

499. Does it impact schedule, cost, quality?

500. What deliverables come first?

2.24 Quality Management Plan: Salesforce CPQ

501. How do you check in-coming sample material?

502. With the five whys method, the team considers why the issue being explored occurred. do others then take that initial answer and ask why?

503. Who do you send data to?

504. Who gets results of work?

505. How effectively was the Quality Management Plan applied during Salesforce CPQ project Execution?

506. Was trending evident between reviews?

507. Do you keep back-up copies of any data?

508. Have all stakeholders been identified?

509. How is equipment calibrated?

510. Who is responsible?

511. How does your organization use comparative data and information to improve organizational performance?

512. Who is responsible for writing the qapp?

513. How does your organization address regulatory,

legal, and ethical compliance?

514. What type of in-house testing do you conduct?

515. Has a Salesforce CPQ project Communications Plan been developed?

516. What is positive about the current process?

517. Contradictory information between document sections?

518. Is the steering committee active in Salesforce CPQ project oversight?

519. What is the return on investment?

520. Are you following the quality standards?

2.25 Quality Metrics: Salesforce CPQ

521. How do you communicate results and findings to upper management?

522. Filter visualizations of interest?

523. Have alternatives been defined in the event that failure occurs?

524. Is there alignment within your organization on definitions?

525. Has it met internal or external standards?

526. Why is now the time for quality metrics?

527. How can the effectiveness of each of the activities be measured?

528. Do you stratify metrics by product or site?

529. Is quality culture a competitive advantage?

530. Product Availability ?

531. The metrics–what is being considered?

532. How do you know if everyone is trying to improve the right things?

533. Was review conducted per standard protocols?

534. What metrics do you measure?

535. What is the CMS Benchmark?

536. How are requirements conflicts resolved?

537. What documentation is required?

538. What metrics are important and most beneficial to measure?

539. Can visual measures help you to filter visualizations of interest?

540. Where is quality now?

2.26 Process Improvement Plan: Salesforce CPQ

541. If a process improvement framework is being used, which elements will help the problems and goals listed?

542. How do you manage quality?

543. Have the frequency of collection and the points in the process where measurements will be made been determined?

544. What actions are needed to address the problems and achieve the goals?

545. What personnel are the champions for the initiative?

546. Who should prepare the process improvement action plan?

547. What makes people good SPI coaches?

548. Why do you want to achieve the goal?

549. Have the supporting tools been developed or acquired?

550. Why quality management?

551. Where do you focus?

552. Are you making progress on your improvement plan?

553. Has the time line required to move measurement results from the points of collection to databases or users been established?

554. Where do you want to be?

555. Does your process ensure quality?

556. Modeling current processes is great, and will you ever see a return on that investment?

557. Are you making progress on the goals?

558. Purpose of goal: the motive is determined by asking, why do you want to achieve this goal?

559. Has a process guide to collect the data been developed?

560. What lessons have you learned so far?

2.27 Responsibility Assignment Matrix: Salesforce CPQ

561. Are work packages assigned to performing organizations?

562. Do others have the time to dedicate to your Salesforce CPQ project?

563. Are overhead costs budgets established on a basis consistent with anticipated direct business base?

564. Are management actions taken to reduce indirect costs when there are significant adverse variances?

565. Incurrence of actual indirect costs in excess of budgets, by element of expense?

566. Changes in the current direct and Salesforce CPQ projected base?

567. What travel needed?

568. Do you know how your people are allocated?

569. Does the contractors system include procedures for measuring the performance of critical subcontractors?

570. Most people let you know when others re too busy, and are others really too busy?

571. Are the wbs and organizational levels for application of the Salesforce CPQ projected overhead costs identified?

572. Is every signing-off responsibility and every communicating responsibility critically necessary?

573. Too many is: do all the identified roles need to be routinely informed or only in exceptional circumstances?

574. Does the accounting system provide a basis for auditing records of direct costs chargeable to the contract?

575. Do managers and team members provide helpful suggestions during review meetings?

576. With too many people labeled as doing the work, are there too many hands involved?

577. Are overhead cost budgets established for each organization which has authority to incur overhead costs?

578. What is the number one predictor of a groups productivity?

2.28 Roles and Responsibilities: Salesforce CPQ

579. What areas of supervision are challenging for you?

580. Do you take the time to clearly define roles and responsibilities on Salesforce CPQ project tasks?

581. Implementation of actions: Who are the responsible units?

582. Attainable / achievable: the goal is attainable; can you actually accomplish the goal?

583. Who: who is involved?

584. Are Salesforce CPQ project team roles and responsibilities identified and documented?

585. What expectations were NOT met?

586. Are governance roles and responsibilities documented?

587. What specific behaviors did you observe?

588. What should you do now to prepare yourself for a promotion, increased responsibilities or a different job?

589. How well did the Salesforce CPQ project Team understand the expectations of specific roles and

responsibilities?

590. Once the responsibilities are defined for the Salesforce CPQ project, have the deliverables, roles and responsibilities been clearly communicated to every participant?

591. How is your work-life balance?

592. To decide whether to use a quality measurement, ask how will you know when it is achieved?

593. Where are you most strong as a supervisor?

594. Does the team have access to and ability to use data analysis tools?

595. Key conclusions and recommendations: Are conclusions and recommendations relevant and acceptable?

596. What are your major roles and responsibilities in the area of performance measurement and assessment?

2.29 Human Resource Management Plan: Salesforce CPQ

597. Identify who is needed on the core Salesforce CPQ project team to complete Salesforce CPQ project deliverables and achieve its goals and objectives. What skills, knowledge and experiences are required?

598. Has a resource management plan been created?

599. Is a stakeholder management plan in place that covers topics?

600. Who needs training?

601. Has a quality assurance plan been developed for the Salesforce CPQ project?

602. Are metrics used to evaluate and manage Vendors?

603. What did you have to assume to be true to complete the charter?

604. What is this Salesforce CPQ project aiming to achieve?

605. Has the business need been clearly defined?

606. Sensitivity analysis?

607. Are risk oriented checklists used during risk identification?

608. Are non-critical path items updated and agreed upon with the teams?

609. Is there a formal process for updating the Salesforce CPQ project baseline?

610. How do you determine what key skills and talents are needed to meet the objectives. Is your organization primarily focused on a specific industry?

611. Have reserves been created to address risks?

612. What areas does the group agree are the biggest success on the Salesforce CPQ project?

613. Pareto diagrams, statistical sampling, flow charting or trend analysis used quality monitoring?

614. Has the Salesforce CPQ project scope been baselined?

615. Have stakeholder accountabilities & responsibilities been clearly defined?

2.30 Communications Management Plan: Salesforce CPQ

616. What are the interrelationships?

617. Are others needed?

618. Where do team members get information?

619. Are there common objectives between the team and the stakeholder?

620. Why manage stakeholders?

621. Why do you manage communications?

622. Who are the members of the governing body?

623. Do you prepare stakeholder engagement plans?

624. What steps can you take for a positive relationship?

625. What is the stakeholders level of authority?

626. What is the political influence?

627. Who did you turn to if you had questions?

628. What data is going to be required?

629. Will messages be directly related to the release strategy or phases of the Salesforce CPQ project?

630. Do you have members of your team responsible for certain stakeholders?

631. Why is stakeholder engagement important?

632. Which stakeholders are thought leaders, influences, or early adopters?

633. Can you think of other people who might have concerns or interests?

634. Which stakeholders can influence others?

635. Who needs to know and how much?

2.31 Risk Management Plan: Salesforce CPQ

636. Risk may be made during which step of risk management?

637. Costs associated with late delivery or a defective product?

638. What things might go wrong?

639. Financial risk: can your organization afford to undertake the Salesforce CPQ project?

640. What will the damage be?

641. Does the Salesforce CPQ project have the authority and ability to avoid the risk?

642. Prioritized components/features?

643. How is risk monitoring performed?

644. Risk documentation: what reporting formats and processes will be used for risk management activities?

645. Workarounds are determined during which step of risk management?

646. Are there risks to human health or the environment that need to be controlled or mitigated?

647. What will drive change?

648. Risk probability and impact: how will the probabilities and impacts of risk items be assessed?

649. Are the reports useful and easy to read?

650. What is the likelihood?

651. Which risks should get the attention?

652. Maximize short-term return on investment?

653. Do requirements put excessive performance constraints on the product?

654. Are formal technical reviews part of this process?

655. What would you do?

2.32 Risk Register: Salesforce CPQ

656. Market risk -will the new service or product be useful to your organization or marketable to others?

657. How is a Community Risk Register created?

658. Is further information required before making a decision?

659. Assume the risk event or situation happens, what would the impact be?

660. What risks might negatively or positively affect achieving the Salesforce CPQ project objectives?

661. What further options might be available for responding to the risk?

662. What are you going to do to limit the Salesforce CPQ projects risk exposure due to the identified risks?

663. What evidence do you have to justify the likelihood score of the risk (audit, incident report, claim, complaints, inspection, internal review)?

664. When would you develop a risk register?

665. Budget and schedule: what are the estimated costs and schedules for performing risk-related activities?

666. Technology risk -is the Salesforce CPQ project technically feasible?

667. How are risks identified?

668. Does the evidence highlight any areas to advance opportunities or foster good relations. If yes what steps will be taken?

669. What is a Community Risk Register?

670. Who is going to do it?

671. Who is accountable?

672. What is a Risk?

673. Schedule impact/severity estimated range (workdays) assume the event happens, what is the potential impact?

674. How are risks graded?

675. Have other controls and solutions been implemented in other services which could be applied as an alternative to additional funding?

2.33 Probability and Impact Assessment: Salesforce CPQ

676. Is the delay in one subSalesforce CPQ project going to affect another?

677. Will there be an increase in the political conservatism?

678. How are the local factors going to affect the absorption?

679. Can it be enlarged by drawing people from other areas of your organization?

680. Are the facilities, expertise, resources, and management know-how available to handle the situation?

681. What will be the likely political environment during the life of the Salesforce CPQ project?

682. Mitigation -how can you avoid the risk?

683. My Salesforce CPQ project leader has suddenly left your organization, what do you do?

684. Do you train all developers in the process?

685. Which role do you have in the Salesforce CPQ project?

686. What would be the effect of slippage?

687. What will be the environmental impact of the Salesforce CPQ project?

688. Do you use any methods to analyze risks?

689. Your customers business requirements have suddenly shifted because of a new regulatory statute, what now?

690. How do you define a risk?

691. Are the risk data complete?

692. How much risk do others need to take?

693. How do the products attain the specifications?

694. Are tools for analysis and design available?

2.34 Probability and Impact Matrix: Salesforce CPQ

695. How well were you able to manage your risk?

696. What are data sources?

697. Does the customer understand the software process?

698. How can you understand and diagnose risks and identify sources?

699. What is the likely future demand of the customer?

700. Sensitivity analysis -which risks will have the most impact on the Salesforce CPQ project?

701. Can you avoid altogether some things that might go wrong?

702. Do others match with the clients requirement?

703. How realistic is the timing of introduction?

704. Lay ground work for future returns?

705. Are team members trained in the use of the tools?

706. Number of users of the product?

707. Workarounds are determined during which risk management process?

708. Is the customer willing to participate in reviews?

709. What kind of preparation would be required to do this?

710. How much is the probability of the risk occurring?

2.35 Risk Data Sheet: Salesforce CPQ

711. What can you do?

712. What is the environment within which you operate (social trends, economic, community values, broad based participation, national directions etc.)?

713. Risk of what?

714. What was measured?

715. What is the chance that it will happen?

716. What will be the consequences if it happens?

717. What were the Causes that contributed?

718. Who has a vested interest in how you perform as your organization (our stakeholders)?

719. What actions can be taken to eliminate or remove risk?

720. Is the data sufficiently specified in terms of the type of failure being analyzed, and its frequency or probability?

721. How reliable is the data source?

722. Are new hazards created?

723. What do you know?

724. What are you here for (Mission)?

725. Has a sensitivity analysis been carried out?

726. Whom do you serve (customers)?

727. If it happens, what are the consequences?

728. Will revised controls lead to tolerable risk levels?

729. Type of risk identified?

2.36 Procurement Management Plan: Salesforce CPQ

730. Has a quality assurance plan been developed for the Salesforce CPQ project?

731. Based on your Salesforce CPQ project communication management plan, what worked well?

732. Is there a procurement management plan in place?

733. Is there a Steering Committee in place?

734. How and when do you enter into Salesforce CPQ project Procurement Management?

735. Was the Salesforce CPQ project schedule reviewed by all stakeholders and formally accepted?

736. What areas does the group agree are the biggest success on the Salesforce CPQ project?

737. Is there a Quality Management Plan?

738. Is documentation created for communication with the suppliers and Vendors?

739. Salesforce CPQ project Objectives?

740. Is the steering committee active in Salesforce CPQ project oversight?

741. Are risk triggers captured?

742. Specific - is the objective clear in terms of what, how, when, and where the situation will be changed?

743. Have Salesforce CPQ project team accountabilities & responsibilities been clearly defined?

744. Were Salesforce CPQ project team members involved in the development of activity & task decomposition?

745. Is there an onboarding process in place?

746. Public engagement – did you get it right?

747. Does the Salesforce CPQ project have a Statement of Work?

2.37 Source Selection Criteria: Salesforce CPQ

748. What are the guiding principles for developing an evaluation report?

749. How long will it take for the purchase cost to be the same as the lease cost?

750. Is this a cost contract?

751. Who should attend debriefings?

752. What are the most critical evaluation criteria that prove to be tiebreakers in the evaluation of proposals?

753. Are responses to considerations adequate?

754. When is it appropriate to conduct a preproposal conference?

755. How should the solicitation aspects regarding past performance be structured?

756. Team leads: what is your process for assigning ratings?

757. Who is on the Source Selection Advisory Committee?

758. Will the technical evaluation factor unnecessarily force the acquisition into a higher-priced market segment?

759. What source selection software is your team using?

760. In the technical/management area, what criteria do you use to determine the final evaluation ratings?

761. What should preproposal conferences accomplish?

762. How is past performance evaluated?

763. Are there any common areas of weaknesses or deficiencies in the proposals in the competitive range?

764. What are the special considerations for preaward debriefings?

765. What information may not be provided?

766. What common questions or problems are associated with debriefings?

767. Can you reasonably estimate total organization requirements for the coming year?

2.38 Stakeholder Management Plan: Salesforce CPQ

768. Does the business case include how the Salesforce CPQ project aligns with your organizations strategic goals & objectives?

769. Are mitigation strategies identified?

770. Is there a formal set of procedures supporting Issues Management?

771. Which impacts could serve as impediments?

772. Are communication systems currently in place appropriate?

773. Does this include subcontracted development?

774. What specific resources will be required for implementation activities?

775. Are decisions captured in a decisions log?

776. Are the appropriate IT resources adequate to meet planned commitments?

777. Have Salesforce CPQ project team accountabilities & responsibilities been clearly defined?

778. Are multiple estimation methods being employed?

779. Has the schedule been baselined?

780. Are there procedures in place to effectively manage interdependencies with other Salesforce CPQ projects / systems?

781. Are estimating assumptions and constraints captured?

782. Does the Salesforce CPQ project have a formal Salesforce CPQ project Charter?

783. Have all involved Salesforce CPQ project stakeholders and work groups committed to the Salesforce CPQ project?

784. Are schedule deliverables actually delivered?

785. Who is responsible for gathering and reporting data for employment?

786. Is pert / critical path or equivalent methodology being used?

2.39 Change Management Plan: Salesforce CPQ

787. Why is it important?

788. What risks may occur upfront?

789. Will all field readiness criteria have been practically met prior to training roll-out?

790. Who might present the most resistance?

791. What are the needs, priorities and special interests of the audience?

792. What will be the preferred method of delivery?

793. Is there a support model for this application and are the details available for distribution?

794. How much Salesforce CPQ project management is needed?

795. How do you gain sponsors buy-in to the communication plan?

796. How will the stakeholders share information and transfer knowledge?

797. Is there support for this application(s) and are the details available for distribution?

798. How far reaching in your organization is the

change?

799. Where will the funds come from?

800. Have the business unit contacts been selected and notified?

801. Clearly articulate the overall business benefits of the Salesforce CPQ project -why are you doing this now?

802. Is there a software application relevant to this deliverable?

803. What are the training strategies?

804. What roles within your organization are affected, and how?

805. Do you need a new organizational structure?

806. Has the training co-ordinator been provided with the training details and put in place the necessary arrangements?

3.0 Executing Process Group: Salesforce CPQ

807. Do your results resemble a normal distribution?

808. What are deliverables of your Salesforce CPQ project?

809. Who will provide training?

810. It under budget or over budget?

811. Is the Salesforce CPQ project making progress in helping to achieve the set results?

812. What are the typical Salesforce CPQ project management skills?

813. Is the program supported by national and/or local organizations?

814. What type of people would you want on your team?

815. What are the main types of goods and services being outsourced?

816. If action is called for, what form should it take?

817. What were things that you did very well and want to do the same again on the next Salesforce CPQ project?

818. How do you control progress of your Salesforce CPQ project?

819. Who are the Salesforce CPQ project stakeholders?

820. How is Salesforce CPQ project performance information created and distributed?

821. How does Salesforce CPQ project management relate to other disciplines?

822. How well did the chosen processes produce the expected results?

823. Mitigate. what will you do to minimize the impact should a risk event occur?

3.1 Team Member Status Report: Salesforce CPQ

824. When a teams productivity and success depend on collaboration and the efficient flow of information, what generally fails them?

825. Are the products of your organizations Salesforce CPQ projects meeting customers objectives?

826. Why is it to be done?

827. How will resource planning be done?

828. Is there evidence that staff is taking a more professional approach toward management of your organizations Salesforce CPQ projects?

829. How does this product, good, or service meet the needs of the Salesforce CPQ project and your organization as a whole?

830. Do you have an Enterprise Salesforce CPQ project Management Office (EPMO)?

831. Does every department have to have a Salesforce CPQ project Manager on staff?

832. Does your organization have the means (staff, money, contract, etc.) to produce or to acquire the product, good, or service?

833. How can you make it practical?

834. Are the attitudes of staff regarding Salesforce CPQ project work improving?

835. How it is to be done?

836. The problem with Reward & Recognition Programs is that the truly deserving people all too often get left out. How can you make it practical?

837. What is to be done?

838. Are your organizations Salesforce CPQ projects more successful over time?

839. Does the product, good, or service already exist within your organization?

840. How much risk is involved?

841. What specific interest groups do you have in place?

842. Will the staff do training or is that done by a third party?

3.2 Change Request: Salesforce CPQ

843. What is a Change Request Form?

844. Should a more thorough impact analysis be conducted?

845. When do you create a change request?

846. Screen shots or attachments included in a Change Request?

847. How are changes graded and who is responsible for the rating?

848. Who needs to approve change requests?

849. How fast will change requests be approved?

850. Can static requirements change attributes like the size of the change be used to predict reliability in execution?

851. How is the change documented (format, content, storage)?

852. How can changes be graded?

853. Who can suggest changes?

854. Describe how modifications, enhancements, defects and/or deficiencies shall be notified (e.g. Problem Reports, Change Requests etc) and managed. Detail warranty and/or maintenance

periods?

855. How to get changes (code) out in a timely manner?

856. How does a team identify the discrete elements of a configuration?

857. Are there requirements attributes that are strongly related to the occurrence of defects and failures?

858. How does your organization control changes before and after software is released to a customer?

859. Why control change across the life cycle?

860. Should staff call into the helpdesk or go to the website?

861. Is it feasible to use requirements attributes as predictors of reliability?

862. Why do you want to have a change control system?

3.3 Change Log: Salesforce CPQ

863. How does this change affect scope?

864. Is this a mandatory replacement?

865. When was the request approved?

866. Is the change backward compatible without limitations?

867. Is the submitted change a new change or a modification of a previously approved change?

868. Do the described changes impact on the integrity or security of the system?

869. Is the requested change request a result of changes in other Salesforce CPQ project(s)?

870. How does this relate to the standards developed for specific business processes?

871. Will the Salesforce CPQ project fail if the change request is not executed?

872. How does this change affect the timeline of the schedule?

873. Who initiated the change request?

874. Is the change request open, closed or pending?

875. Is the change request within Salesforce CPQ

project scope?

876. When was the request submitted?

3.4 Decision Log: Salesforce CPQ

877. Who is the decisionmaker?

878. What is the average size of your matters in an applicable measurement?

879. Behaviors; what are guidelines that the team has identified that will assist them with getting the most out of team meetings?

880. Meeting purpose; why does this team meet?

881. At what point in time does loss become unacceptable?

882. How do you define success?

883. Does anything need to be adjusted?

884. How does provision of information, both in terms of content and presentation, influence acceptance of alternative strategies?

885. What was the rationale for the decision?

886. What alternatives/risks were considered?

887. Is everything working as expected?

888. Which variables make a critical difference?

889. What is the line where eDiscovery ends and document review begins?

890. Decision-making process; how will the team make decisions?

891. How do you know when you are achieving it?

892. Adversarial environment. is your opponent open to a non-traditional workflow, or will it likely challenge anything you do?

893. It becomes critical to track and periodically revisit both operational effectiveness; Are you noticing all that you need to, and are you interpreting what you see effectively?

894. How does the use a Decision Support System influence the strategies/tactics or costs?

895. What are the cost implications?

896. Linked to original objective?

3.5 Quality Audit: Salesforce CPQ

897. Is your organizations resource allocation system properly aligned with its collection of intentions?

898. Is there a risk that information provided by management may not always be reliable?

899. How do you know what, specifically, is required of you in your work?

900. Is there a written procedure for receiving materials?

901. How does your organization know that its staff are presenting original work, and properly acknowledging the work of others?

902. Are all employees including salespersons made aware that they must report all complaints received from any source for inclusion in the complaint handling system?

903. How does your organization know that its general support services planning and management systems are appropriately effective and constructive?

904. Are all records associated with the reconditioning of a device maintained for a minimum of two years after the sale or disposal of the last device within a lot of merchandise?

905. Are the policies and processes, as set out in the Quality Audit Manual, properly applied?

906. Does the audit organization have experience in performing the required work for entities of your type and size?

907. Is there a written corporate quality policy?

908. How does your organization know that its management of its ethical responsibilities is appropriately effective and constructive?

909. How does your organization know that its relationships with industry and employers are appropriately effective and constructive?

910. How does your organization know that it is appropriately effective and constructive in preparing its staff for organizational aspirations?

911. How does your organization know that the system for managing its facilities is appropriately effective and constructive?

912. How does your organization know that its relationship with its (past) staff is appropriately effective and constructive?

913. Are there appropriate indicators for monitoring the effectiveness and efficiency of processes?

914. How does your organization know that its systems for assisting staff with career planning and employment placements are appropriately effective and constructive?

915. Quality is about improvement and accountability.

The immediate questions that arise out of that statement are: (i) improvement on what, and (ii) accountable to whom?

916. What does an analysis of your organizations staff profile suggest in terms of its planning, and how is this being addressed?

3.6 Team Directory: Salesforce CPQ

917. How will the team handle changes?

918. Who will be the stakeholders on your next Salesforce CPQ project?

919. How does the team resolve conflicts and ensure tasks are completed?

920. What needs to be communicated?

921. Where will the product be used and/or delivered or built when appropriate?

922. Decisions: what could be done better to improve the quality of the constructed product?

923. Who should receive information (all stakeholders)?

924. Where should the information be distributed?

925. Why is the work necessary?

926. Process decisions: do job conditions warrant additional actions to collect job information and document on-site activity?

927. Who are the Team Members?

928. Days from the time the issue is identified?

929. Contract requirements complied with?

930. How and in what format should information be presented?

931. Process decisions: are contractors adequately prosecuting the work?

932. Process decisions: do invoice amounts match accepted work in place?

933. Who will report Salesforce CPQ project status to all stakeholders?

934. How do unidentified risks impact the outcome of the Salesforce CPQ project?

3.7 Team Operating Agreement: Salesforce CPQ

935. What types of accommodations will be formulated and put in place for sustaining the team?

936. Why does your organization want to participate in teaming?

937. Are there more than two national cultures represented by your team?

938. How will you divide work equitably?

939. Did you recap the meeting purpose, time, and expectations?

940. Do team members need to frequently communicate as a full group to make timely decisions?

941. Do you send out the agenda and meeting materials in advance?

942. Are there differences in access to communication and collaboration technology based on team member location?

943. How will you resolve conflict efficiently and respectfully?

944. What individual strengths does each team member bring to the group?

945. To whom do you deliver your services?

946. Do you determine the meeting length and time of day?

947. How does teaming fit in with overall organizational goals and meet organizational needs?

948. Has the appropriate access to relevant data and analysis capability been granted?

949. Have you established procedures that team members can follow to work effectively together, such as a team operating agreement?

950. What are the current caseload numbers in the unit?

951. Methodologies: how will key team processes be implemented, such as training, research, work deliverable production, review and approval processes, knowledge management, and meeting procedures?

952. Do you record meetings for the already stated unable to attend?

953. Did you determine the technology methods that best match the messages to be communicated?

3.8 Team Performance Assessment: Salesforce CPQ

954. When a reviewer complains about method variance, what is the essence of the complaint?

955. How hard did you try to make a good selection?

956. To what degree do team members understand one anothers roles and skills?

957. How do you keep key people outside the group informed about its accomplishments?

958. To what degree are sub-teams possible or necessary?

959. To what degree does the teams work approach provide opportunity for members to engage in open interaction?

960. How do you recognize and praise members for contributions?

961. To what degree are the relative importance and priority of the goals clear to all team members?

962. Do you give group members authority to make at least some important decisions?

963. Is there a particular method of data analysis that you would recommend as a means of demonstrating that method variance is not of great concern for a

given dataset?

964. To what degree will the approach capitalize on and enhance the skills of all team members in a manner that takes into consideration other demands on members of the team?

965. To what degree do all members feel responsible for all agreed-upon measures?

966. If you have received criticism from reviewers that your work suffered from method variance, what was the circumstance?

967. If you are worried about method variance before you collect data, what sort of design elements might you include to reduce or eliminate the threat of method variance?

968. To what degree does the teams purpose constitute a broader, deeper aspiration than just accomplishing short-term goals?

969. To what degree are the goals ambitious?

970. To what degree are fresh input and perspectives systematically caught and added (for example, through information and analysis, new members, and senior sponsors)?

971. To what degree are the goals realistic?

972. When does the medium matter?

973. What are you doing specifically to develop the leaders around you?

3.9 Team Member Performance Assessment: Salesforce CPQ

974. How do you use data to inform instruction and improve staff achievement?

975. To what degree do team members feel that the purpose of the team is important, if not exciting?

976. Does adaptive training work?

977. How are assessments designed, delivered, and otherwise used to maximize training?

978. What is a significant fact or event?

979. What is the Business Management Oversight Process?

980. How does your team work together?

981. Is it critical or vital to the job?

982. Does the rater (supervisor) have to wait for the interim or final performance assessment review to tell an employee that the employees performance is unsatisfactory?

983. Does the rater (supervisor) have the authority or responsibility to tell an employee that the employees performance is unsatisfactory?

984. To what degree is the team cognizant of small

wins to be celebrated along the way?

985. How often are assessments to be conducted?

986. What is the target group for instruction (e.g., individual and collective or small team instruction)?

987. How often should assessments be conducted?

988. How will you identify your Team Leaders?

989. Why do performance reviews?

990. What future plans (e.g., modifications) do you have for your program?

991. What is a general description of the processes under performance measurement and assessment?

992. How are performance measures and associated incentives developed?

993. Why were corresponding selected?

3.10 Issue Log: Salesforce CPQ

994. Do you often overlook a key stakeholder or stakeholder group?

995. How often do you engage with stakeholders?

996. In classifying stakeholders, which approach to do so are you using?

997. What does the stakeholder need from the team?

998. What help do you and your team need from the stakeholders?

999. Is access to the Issue Log controlled?

1000. How is this initiative related to other portfolios, programs, or Salesforce CPQ projects?

1001. Which team member will work with each stakeholder?

1002. Can an impact cause deviation beyond team, stage or Salesforce CPQ project tolerances?

1003. Are stakeholder roles recognized by your organization?

1004. Are the Salesforce CPQ project issues uniquely identified, including to which product they refer?

1005. Persistence; will users learn a work around or will they be bothered every time?

1006. What effort will a change need?

1007. How do you manage communications?

1008. Who is involved as you identify stakeholders?

4.0 Monitoring and Controlling Process Group: Salesforce CPQ

1009. Accuracy: what design will lead to accurate information?

1010. How is agile Salesforce CPQ project management done?

1011. How to ensure validity, quality and consistency?

1012. If a risk event occurs, what will you do?

1013. Is there sufficient time allotted between the general system design and the detailed system design phases?

1014. What kinds of things in particular are you looking for data on?

1015. What input will you be required to provide the Salesforce CPQ project team?

1016. Are the services being delivered?

1017. Were escalated issues resolved promptly?

1018. How should needs be met?

1019. Were decisions made in a timely manner?

1020. Did the Salesforce CPQ project team have enough people to execute the Salesforce CPQ project plan?

1021. Did you implement the program as designed?

1022. What areas does the group agree are the biggest success on the Salesforce CPQ project?

1023. What is the timeline?

1024. What will you do to minimize the impact should a risk event occur?

4.1 Project Performance Report: Salesforce CPQ

1025. To what degree does the teams approach to its work allow for modification and improvement over time?

1026. To what degree are the demands of the task compatible with and converge with the relationships of the informal organization?

1027. To what degree will each member have the opportunity to advance his or her professional skills in all three of the above categories while contributing to the accomplishment of the teams purpose and goals?

1028. What is the PRS?

1029. To what degree are the teams goals and objectives clear, simple, and measurable?

1030. How can Salesforce CPQ project sustainability be maintained?

1031. To what degree do members articulate the goals beyond the team membership?

1032. To what degree does the funding match the requirement?

1033. Next Steps?

1034. To what degree does the information network

provide individuals with the information they require?

1035. To what degree is there a sense that only the team can succeed?

1036. To what degree will the team adopt a concrete, clearly understood, and agreed-upon approach that will result in achievement of the teams goals?

1037. To what degree do the structures of the formal organization motivate taskrelevant behavior and facilitate task completion?

1038. To what degree will new and supplemental skills be introduced as the need is recognized?

1039. To what degree do team members frequently explore the teams purpose and its implications?

4.2 Variance Analysis: Salesforce CPQ

1040. Did a new competitor enter the market?

1041. At what point should variances be isolated and brought to the attention of the management?

1042. Why do variances exist?

1043. Are the bases and rates for allocating costs from each indirect pool consistently applied?

1044. What was the cause of the increase in costs?

1045. Does the contractors system provide unit or lot costs when applicable?

1046. What is the dollar amount of the fluctuation?

1047. Why are standard cost systems used?

1048. Did an existing competitor change strategy?

1049. What does a favorable labor efficiency variance mean?

1050. What does an unfavorable overhead volume variance mean?

1051. How does the use of a single conversion element (rather than the traditional labor and overhead elements) affect standard costing?

1052. What is your organizations rationale for sharing

expenses and services between business segments?

1053. Do the rates and prices remain constant throughout the year?

1054. What is the expected future profitability of each customer?

1055. Favorable or unfavorable variance?

1056. Other relevant issues of Variance Analysis -selling price or gross margin?

1057. What costs are avoidable if one or more customers are dropped?

4.3 Earned Value Status: Salesforce CPQ

1058. If earned value management (EVM) is so good in determining the true status of a Salesforce CPQ project and Salesforce CPQ project its completion, why is it that hardly any one uses it in information systems related Salesforce CPQ projects?

1059. Verification is a process of ensuring that the developed system satisfies the stakeholders agreements and specifications; Are you building the product right? What do you verify?

1060. Are you hitting your Salesforce CPQ projects targets?

1061. Where is evidence-based earned value in your organization reported?

1062. What is the unit of forecast value?

1063. How much is it going to cost by the finish?

1064. Where are your problem areas?

1065. Earned value can be used in almost any Salesforce CPQ project situation and in almost any Salesforce CPQ project environment. it may be used on large Salesforce CPQ projects, medium sized Salesforce CPQ projects, tiny Salesforce CPQ projects (in cut-down form), complex and simple Salesforce CPQ projects and in any market sector. some people, of course, know all about earned value, they have used it for years - but perhaps not as effectively as they could have?

1066. Validation is a process of ensuring that the developed system will actually achieve the stakeholders desired outcomes; Are you building the right product? What do you validate?

1067. How does this compare with other Salesforce CPQ projects?

1068. When is it going to finish?

4.4 Risk Audit: Salesforce CPQ

1069. What are the strategic implications with clients when auditors focus audit resources based on business-level risks?

1070. Can analytical tests provide evidence that is as strong as evidence from traditional substantive tests?

1071. Do requirements demand the use of new analysis, design, or testing methods?

1072. How risk averse are you?

1073. What responsibilities for quality, errors, and outcomes have been delegated to staff (or others) without adequate oversight?

1074. Do you promote education and training opportunities?

1075. Do you meet all obligations relating to funds secured from grants, loans and sponsors?

1076. If applicable; which route/packaging option do you choose for transport of hazmat material?

1077. What are the Internal Controls ?

1078. Does your organization have or has considered the need for insurance covers: public liability, professional indemnity and directors and officers liability?

1079. Have customers been involved fully in the definition of requirements?

1080. What is the implication of budget constraint on this process?

1081. Have reasonable steps been taken to reduce the risks to acceptable levels?

1082. The halo effect in business risk audits: can strategic risk assessment bias auditor judgment about accounting details?

1083. What expertise does the Board have on quality, outcomes, and errors?

1084. Do you have a mechanism for managing change?

1085. Do you have a procedure for dealing with complaints?

1086. For paid staff, does your organization comply with the minimum conditions for employment and/or the applicable modern award?

1087. Does your organization have a register of insurance policies detailing all current insurance policies?

1088. Are auditors able to effectively apply more soft evidence found in the risk-assessment process with the results of more tangible audit evidence found through more substantive testing?

4.5 Contractor Status Report: Salesforce CPQ

1089. How long have you been using the services?

1090. Describe how often regular updates are made to the proposed solution. Are corresponding regular updates included in the standard maintenance plan?

1091. Who can list a Salesforce CPQ project as organization experience, your organization or a previous employee of your organization?

1092. What was the budget or estimated cost for your organizations services?

1093. How does the proposed individual meet each requirement?

1094. What was the final actual cost?

1095. What is the average response time for answering a support call?

1096. What was the overall budget or estimated cost?

1097. How is risk transferred?

1098. If applicable; describe your standard schedule for new software version releases. Are new software version releases included in the standard maintenance plan?

1099. What process manages the contracts?

1100. What are the minimum and optimal bandwidth requirements for the proposed solution?

1101. What was the actual budget or estimated cost for your organizations services?

1102. Are there contractual transfer concerns?

4.6 Formal Acceptance: Salesforce CPQ

1103. Did the Salesforce CPQ project manager and team act in a professional and ethical manner?

1104. Do you perform formal acceptance or burn-in tests?

1105. General estimate of the costs and times to complete the Salesforce CPQ project?

1106. Is formal acceptance of the Salesforce CPQ project product documented and distributed?

1107. Who supplies data?

1108. What features, practices, and processes proved to be strengths or weaknesses?

1109. What are the requirements against which to test, Who will execute?

1110. How well did the team follow the methodology?

1111. What lessons were learned about your Salesforce CPQ project management methodology?

1112. What is the Acceptance Management Process?

1113. Was the sponsor/customer satisfied?

1114. Have all comments been addressed?

1115. What function(s) does it fill or meet?

1116. Was the Salesforce CPQ project managed well?

1117. What was done right?

1118. Do you buy-in installation services?

1119. Was the Salesforce CPQ project work done on time, within budget, and according to specification?

1120. How does your team plan to obtain formal acceptance on your Salesforce CPQ project?

1121. Does it do what Salesforce CPQ project team said it would?

1122. Was the Salesforce CPQ project goal achieved?

5.0 Closing Process Group: Salesforce CPQ

1123. How dependent is the Salesforce CPQ project on other Salesforce CPQ projects or work efforts?

1124. What could be done to improve the process?

1125. Did the Salesforce CPQ project team have the right skills?

1126. Did the delivered product meet the specified requirements and goals of the Salesforce CPQ project?

1127. What level of risk does the proposed budget represent to the Salesforce CPQ project?

1128. What will you do?

1129. Did the Salesforce CPQ project team have enough people to execute the Salesforce CPQ project plan?

1130. What do you need to do?

1131. Is this a follow-on to a previous Salesforce CPQ project?

1132. What communication items need improvement?

1133. What is the amount of funding and what Salesforce CPQ project phases are funded?

1134. Were cost budgets met?

1135. What is the risk of failure to your organization?

1136. Did you do things well?

1137. Was the user/client satisfied with the end product?

5.1 Procurement Audit: Salesforce CPQ

1138. Is sufficient evidence required for all disbursements (except nominal amounts)?

1139. Is your organization policy on purchasing covered by a written manual?

1140. Has guidelines been set up for how the procurement function/unit should carry out its procurements?

1141. Do you learn from benchmarking your own practices with international standards?

1142. Is your organization transparent about winning bids and prices?

1143. How do you avoid delays at any stage/ stages of the procurement process?

1144. Is it on a regular basis examined whether it is possible to enter into public private partnerships with private suppliers?

1145. Has a deputy treasurer been appointed to sign checks when the treasurer is unable to perform that duty?

1146. Can small orders such as magazine subscriptions and non-product items such as membership in organizations be processed by the ordering department?

1147. Is the strategy implemented across the entire organization?

1148. Have the funding arrangements been agreed where payments take place over several financial periods?

1149. Is there no evidence of unauthorized release of information or seemingly unnecessary contacts with bidders personnel during the evaluation and negotiation processes?

1150. Are there mechanisms for evaluating the departments suppliers performance in relation to prices, quality, delivery and innovation?

1151. Are all complaints of late or incorrect payment sent to a person independent of the already stated having cash disbursement responsibilities?

1152. When competitive dialogue was used, did the contracting authority provide sufficient justification for the use of this procedure and was the contract actually particularly complex?

1153. Did your organization state the minimum requirements to be met by the variants in the tender documents?

1154. Were the specifications of the contract determined free from influence of particular interests of consultants, experts or other economic operators?

1155. Are the supporting documents for payments

voided or cancelled following payment?

1156. Are cases of double payment duly prevented and corrected?

1157. Is funding made available for payments under the contract at the appropriate time and in accordance with the relevant national/public financial procedures?

5.2 Contract Close-Out: Salesforce CPQ

1158. Change in circumstances?

1159. Was the contract type appropriate?

1160. How does it work?

1161. Was the contract sufficiently clear so as not to result in numerous disputes and misunderstandings?

1162. What happens to the recipient of services?

1163. Have all contracts been completed?

1164. Why Outsource?

1165. Have all contracts been closed?

1166. Are the signers the authorized officials?

1167. How/when used ?

1168. Was the contract complete without requiring numerous changes and revisions?

1169. What is capture management?

1170. Have all acceptance criteria been met prior to final payment to contractors?

1171. Change in attitude or behavior?

1172. How is the contracting office notified of the automatic contract close-out?

1173. Parties: Authorized?

1174. Have all contract records been included in the Salesforce CPQ project archives?

1175. Has each contract been audited to verify acceptance and delivery?

1176. Parties: who is involved?

1177. Change in knowledge?

5.3 Project or Phase Close-Out: Salesforce CPQ

1178. In addition to assessing whether the Salesforce CPQ project was successful, it is equally critical to analyze why it was or was not fully successful. Are you including this?

1179. When and how were information needs best met?

1180. Was the schedule met?

1181. Is the lesson significant, valid, and applicable?

1182. Does the lesson describe a function that would be done differently the next time?

1183. Planned completion date?

1184. Did the delivered product meet the specified requirements and goals of the Salesforce CPQ project?

1185. Were risks identified and mitigated?

1186. What information is each stakeholder group interested in?

1187. Which changes might a stakeholder be required to make as a result of the Salesforce CPQ project?

1188. What was learned?

1189. Were messages directly related to the release strategy or phases of the Salesforce CPQ project?

1190. What can you do better next time, and what specific actions can you take to improve?

1191. What benefits or impacts does the stakeholder group expect to obtain as a result of the Salesforce CPQ project?

1192. What could have been improved?

1193. Who is responsible for award close-out?

1194. Is there a clear cause and effect between the activity and the lesson learned?

1195. In preparing the Lessons Learned report, should it reflect a consensus viewpoint, or should the report reflect the different individual viewpoints?

1196. What process was planned for managing issues/ risks?

5.4 Lessons Learned: Salesforce CPQ

1197. Who needs to learn lessons?

1198. How was the Salesforce CPQ project controlled?

1199. How many government and contractor personnel are authorized for the Salesforce CPQ project?

1200. Did the Salesforce CPQ project improve the team members reputations, skills, personal development?

1201. How useful was the format and content of the Salesforce CPQ project Status Report to you?

1202. What is the impact of tax policy on the case?

1203. What is your working hypothesis, if you have one?

1204. Was the necessary hardware, software, accommodation etc available?

1205. What would you approach differently next time?

1206. How complete and timely were the materials you were provided to decide whether to proceed from one Salesforce CPQ project lifecycle phase to the next?

1207. How effective was the documentation that you received with the Salesforce CPQ project product/

service?

1208. Were any objectives unmet?

1209. What were the most significant issues on this Salesforce CPQ project?

1210. Who had fiscal authority to manage the funding for the Salesforce CPQ project, did that work?

1211. How efficient is the deliverable?

1212. How effectively and consistently was sponsorship for the Salesforce CPQ project conveyed?

1213. What is your overall assessment of the outcome of this Salesforce CPQ project?

1214. What is the expected lifespan of the deliverable?

1215. How often did you violate the rules?

1216. What is your strategy for data collection?

Index

ability 35, 121, 127, 201, 206
absorption 210
accept 101, 179
acceptable 79, 82, 109, 201, 256
acceptance 8, 26, 150-151, 232, 259-260, 266-267
accepted 145, 216, 238
access 4, 9-11, 19, 33, 75, 94, 104, 112, 124-125, 127, 201, 239-240, 245
accessed 93, 116, 122
accomplish 9, 85, 168, 200, 219
accordance 265
according 29, 32, 119, 161, 260
account 19, 27, 51, 53, 101, 128, 157, 178
accounted 49
accounting 21, 199, 256
accounts 41, 52, 127-128, 162
accrue 148
accuracy 48, 185, 247
accurate 11, 52, 105, 161, 169, 182, 247
accurately 136
achievable 200
achieve 9, 70, 74, 123, 168, 196-197, 202, 224, 254
achieved 22, 136, 201, 260
achieving 126, 208, 233
acquire 226
acquired 196
across 89, 229, 264
action 21, 77, 101, 115, 120, 147, 155, 196, 224
actions 23, 83-85, 196, 198, 200, 214, 237, 269
active 93, 147, 157, 193, 216
activities 33, 79, 103, 105, 115, 126, 130, 149, 164, 166-167, 170, 172-173, 183, 186-187, 194, 206, 208, 220
activity 5-6, 30-31, 66, 144, 164, 166, 168, 170, 172-174, 178, 182, 186, 217, 237, 269
actors 141
actual 31, 161-162, 198, 257-258
actually 37, 70-71, 98, 200, 221, 254, 264
actuals 184
adaptive 243
adding 59

addition 36, 268
additional 26, 33, 47, 53-54, 56, 61-63, 94, 102-103, 114, 188, 209, 237
additions 46, 87
address 1, 71, 114, 129, 164, 183, 192, 196, 203
addressed 144-145, 174, 236, 259
Addresses 94
addressing 35, 116
adequate 147, 155, 165, 218, 220, 255
adequately 33, 238
adhered 162
adjust 82
adjusted 90, 232
adopters 205
advance 162, 209, 239, 249
advantage 1, 47, 92, 95, 115, 194
advantages 141-142
adverse 198
advise 2
Advisory 218
affect 62, 84, 130-131, 136, 153, 208, 210, 230, 251
affected 141, 165, 179, 223
affecting 13, 23, 54
afford 206
against28, 87, 89, 184, 190, 259
agenda 136, 144, 239
agents 115
aggressive 130
agility 42
agreed 40, 45, 127, 149, 203, 264
Agreement 7, 239-240
agreements 147, 184, 253
aiming 202
alerting 149
alerts 87, 98, 115
algorithms 93
aligned 22, 234
alignment 194
aligns 147, 184, 220
alleged 3
allegedly 51, 77
Alliances 141
allied 141

allocate 187
allocated 198
allocating 251
allocation 234
allotted 247
allowable 43
allowed 2, 56, 61, 111, 133, 176
allows 11, 172, 182
almost 253
alongside 112
already 162, 227, 240, 264
altered 128
alternate 102
altogether 212
always 11, 19, 52, 103, 107, 119, 234
ambitious 242
amended 114, 116, 158
amount 23, 251, 261
amounts 127, 238, 263
amplify 56
analysis 4, 7, 11-12, 40-43, 47-48, 54, 56, 58-60, 62, 66, 69, 71, 73, 141, 145, 147, 165, 185, 188, 201-203, 211-212, 215, 228, 236, 240-242, 251-252, 255
analytical 255
Analytics 41, 45
analyze 4, 43-44, 50-51, 63, 69, 184, 211, 268
analyzed 39, 44, 71, 87, 155, 161, 214
annual 190
annually 99
another 96, 115, 160, 210
anothers 241
answer 12-13, 17, 25, 39, 50, 65, 81, 92, 192
answered 24, 38, 49, 64, 79, 91, 134
answering 12, 170, 257
anyone 34
anything 164, 174, 232-233
API-driven 62
appear 3
applicable 12, 150, 161, 232, 251, 255-257, 268
applied 67, 115, 168, 184, 192, 209, 234, 251
appointed 29, 32, 263
appraised 99

approach 69, 95, 104, 108, 116, 119, 129, 165, 186, 226, 241-242, 245, 249-250, 270
approaches 109
approval 53, 97, 106, 240
approvals 89, 149-150
approve 155, 228
approved 95, 145, 150, 153, 157, 164-165, 190, 228, 230
approving 153
architect 155
Architects 9
archives 267
arising 137
around 242, 245
articulate 223, 249
artistic 99
asking 3, 9, 190, 197
aspects 54, 170, 218
aspiration 242
assess 34, 53
assessed 207
assessing 268
assessment 6-7, 10-11, 18, 144, 148, 201, 210, 241, 243-244, 256, 271
assign 58, 104
assigned 27, 35, 59, 112, 127, 145, 155, 159, 161-162, 198
assigning 177, 218
Assignment 6, 169, 198
assist 10, 74, 98, 188, 232
assistant 9, 93, 96
assisting 235
assistive 94
associate 113
associated 109, 206, 219, 234, 244
assume 202, 208-209
Assumption 5, 157
assurance 165, 202, 216
assure 48
attacks 22
attain 211
attainable 32, 200
attempted 34
attend 18, 218, 240
attendance 29, 107

attendant 75, 125
attended 1, 29
attention 13, 207, 251
attitude 266
attitudes 227
attractive 126
attribute 123, 185
attributes 5, 96, 113, 121, 130, 164, 168, 228-229
attrition 113
audience 222
audited 185, 267
auditing 90, 199
auditor 256
auditors 255-256
audits 256
author 3
authority 199, 204, 206, 241, 243, 264, 271
authorized 33, 120, 146, 266-267, 270
automate 45, 57, 77
automatic 103, 267
available 23, 31, 33, 70, 76, 107, 114-115, 126, 129, 131, 136, 146, 161, 167, 176, 182, 186, 208, 210-211, 222, 265, 270
Average 13, 24, 38, 49, 64, 80, 91, 109, 134, 180, 232, 257
averse 255
avoidable 252
awareness 96
background 11, 139
backing 142
back-up 192
backward 230
balance 21, 89, 112, 127, 201
balanced 66
bandwidth 258
baseline 6, 44, 155, 164, 190, 203
baselined 45, 203, 221
baselines 29
because 2, 41, 183, 211
become 150, 153, 232
becomes 233
before 1-2, 11, 34, 53, 93, 104, 118, 166, 172-173, 185, 191, 208, 229, 242
beginning 4, 16, 24, 38, 49, 64, 80, 91, 111, 134
begins 93, 232

behalf 115
behavior 65, 250, 266
behaviors 70, 200, 232
behind 2
belief 12, 17, 25, 39, 50, 65, 81, 92
believe 2
Benchmark 195
benchmarks 82
beneficial 195
benefit 3, 21, 42, 45, 57, 72-73, 79, 88, 98, 115
benefits 19, 40, 42, 54-55, 57, 75, 77, 92, 123, 132-133, 148, 223, 269
better 9, 36, 43, 69, 89, 94, 166, 181, 188, 237, 269
between 41-42, 54-55, 98, 123, 125, 127, 153, 161, 176, 178, 192-193, 204, 247, 252, 269
beyond 61, 245, 249
bidders 264
bigger 52
biggest 203, 216, 248
billed 53, 132
billing 53, 90, 112, 121
booked 125
bothered 245
bottleneck 167
bottom 46
boundaries 37
bounds 37
branch 47
branded 120
Breakdown 5, 67, 159, 176
briefed 32
brings 34
broader 242
broken 57
brought 86, 251
browser 35
budget 2, 67, 89, 97, 136, 166, 180, 182, 186-187, 208, 224, 256-258, 260-261
budgeted 161
budgeting 162
budgets 161-162, 198-199, 262
building 23, 138, 157, 253-254
bundle 100, 102, 128

bundling 73, 113
burdensome 116
burn-in 259
business 2, 9, 11, 18, 23, 41-44, 49, 55-56, 63, 70, 77, 95, 101, 111, 114, 123, 125, 131, 144, 147, 152, 156, 184, 186, 190-191, 198, 202, 211, 220, 223, 230, 243, 252, 256
businesses 112, 116
buyers 133
buy-in 222, 260
buying 59, 111
buyout 145
bypassed 78
calculated 96
calibrated 192
called 224
cancelled 265
cannot 162, 183
capability 40, 70, 240
capable 9, 27, 68, 107
capacity 23, 121, 143
capitalize 242
capture 83, 106, 266
captured 39, 61, 152, 164, 185, 217, 220-221
career 153, 235
carried 215
carrying 67
caseload 240
catching 1
categories 61, 249
category 32, 185
caught 242
caused 3
causes 42, 50, 52, 62-63, 83, 143, 145, 214
causing 23
celebrated 244
center 61, 145
centers 42
centrally 66
certain 23, 70, 205
certified 53
challenge 9, 233
challenges 20, 170
champion 28

champions 196
chance 214
change 7, 17, 31, 47, 51, 75, 79, 88, 96, 105-106, 126, 138-140, 145-146, 149, 155, 164, 169, 183-186, 190-191, 206, 222-223, 228-230, 246, 251, 256, 266-267
changed 31, 70, 148, 151, 183, 189, 217
changes 61, 75, 78, 87, 105, 112, 119, 122, 139, 145-146, 150, 161, 176, 185, 191, 198, 228-230, 237, 266, 268
changing 82
channel 96, 100, 106, 129
channels 115
character 94
charge 57, 102
chargeable 199
charged 77
charges 56, 62
charter 4, 30, 33, 40, 43, 138, 143, 202, 221
charters 26
charting 203
charts 44, 47, 52, 182
checked 51, 83, 85, 90
checklists 10, 202
checks 116, 263
choose 12, 51, 57, 104, 255
chosen 143, 225
circumvent 22
claimed 3
classified 161-162
clearly 12, 17, 25, 39, 50, 65, 81, 92, 107, 200-203, 217, 220, 223, 250
client 35, 99, 129, 262
clients 104, 212, 255
closed 81, 162, 164, 230, 266
closely 11
Close-Out 8, 266-269
Closing 8, 54, 261
clothing 99
Coaches 32, 35, 196
coding 31
cognizant 243
collar 89
collect 42-43, 51, 94, 189, 197, 237, 242
collected 27, 36, 44, 53, 56, 63, 71, 155

collection 39-42, 45, 55, 58, 120, 196-197, 234, 271
collective 244
coming 52, 219
command 83
comment 75
comments 259
Commerce 102, 108
commit 120, 147, 184
commitment 125, 143, 161
committed 33, 164-165, 182, 221
committee 147, 157, 193, 216, 218
commodity 98
common 109, 156, 186, 204, 219
community 150, 180, 188-189, 208-209, 214
companies 3, 88, 123
company 1-2, 9
compare 82, 121, 254
compared 96, 184
comparing 162
comparison 12
compatible 101, 230, 249
compelling 34, 105
competing 94
competitor 2, 251
complains 241
complaint 234, 241
complaints 131, 208, 234, 256, 264
complete 3, 10, 12, 33, 36, 38, 89, 148, 166, 169, 173, 176, 180, 202, 211, 259, 266, 270
completed 13, 29, 31, 53, 99, 113, 167, 172-173, 237, 266
completely 1
completing 159, 173
completion 26, 30, 136, 162, 172-173, 187, 250, 253, 268
complex 9, 32, 35, 62, 145, 157, 253, 264
complexity 46, 124, 131
compliance 1, 23, 138, 158, 193
complied 120, 237
comply 256
components 42, 44, 47, 118, 157, 165, 183, 206
compulsory 34
compute 13
concept 156
concepts 157

concern 241
concerned 128
concerns 2, 22, 205, 258
concise 150
concrete 250
concurrent 126
condition 86, 113, 144
conditions 56, 83, 141, 237, 256
conduct 77, 165, 193, 218
conducted 78, 116, 148, 157, 194, 228, 244
conference 218
confidence 51
confident 173
configure 43, 114, 122, 128
configured 116
confirm 12
conflict106, 126, 141, 239
conflicts 151, 195, 237
confusion 132
conjure 151
connected 183
connection 102, 120
consensus 269
consider 22, 126, 133
considered 20, 23, 194, 232, 255
considers 63, 192
consistent 83, 198
console 24, 125
constant 252
constantly 1
constitute 242
constraint 5, 113, 157, 256
consult 1
consultant 1-2, 9, 187
consulting 2
consumer 55
contact 9, 51-53, 66, 102, 129, 164, 185
contacts 101, 223, 264
contain 81, 146
contained 3, 162
contains 10
content 36, 228, 232, 270
contents 3-4, 10

context 124, 178
continual 82, 84
continue 42, 130
continuing 121
continuous 67
contract 8, 26, 97, 99, 105, 107-108, 112, 161, 172, 184, 199, 218, 226, 237, 264-267
contractor 7, 149, 162, 185, 257, 270
contracts 62, 73, 84, 142, 164, 258, 266
contribute 122-123, 129, 131, 133, 144, 151
control 4, 21, 43, 67, 69, 81-83, 86-89, 136, 141, 146, 155, 161-162, 185, 189, 225, 229
controlled 206, 245, 270
controls 67, 84, 172, 185, 209, 215, 255
converge 249
converse 114, 118
conversion 251
convert 52
converted 105
convey 3
conveyed 271
cooperate 188
copies 192
Copyright 3
corporate 2, 36, 235
correct 39, 81, 122, 182, 184
corrected 265
corrective 83, 147
correlate 130
correspond 10-11
costing 41, 251
counting 167
course 31, 254
coverage 84
covered 136, 263
covering 10, 87
covers 202, 255
create 20, 42, 54, 57, 59, 104, 123, 228
created 34, 56, 71, 98, 127, 136, 140, 143, 202-203, 208, 214, 216, 225
creates 41
creating 9, 102
creation 112

creativity 79
credible 132, 188
crisis 21
criteria 4, 6, 10-11, 21, 32, 37, 46, 74, 135-136, 142, 150-151, 153, 188, 218-219, 222, 266
CRITERION 4, 17, 25, 39, 50, 65, 81, 92, 148
critical 21, 36, 52, 56, 84, 89, 132, 167, 170-171, 198, 218, 221, 232-233, 243, 268
critically 199
criticism 242
Crosby 179
crucial 60, 141, 170
crystal 12
cultural70
culture 26, 54, 113, 144, 184, 194
cultures 239
currency 110
current 20, 36, 39, 41, 48, 54-55, 61, 70, 89, 107, 110, 147-148, 15[illegible], 164, 172, 193, 197-198, 240, 256
currently 29, 77, 85, 94, 105, 108, 116, 129-130, 161, 220
custom31, 83, 106, 117, 120
customer 18, 21, 25-27, 30, 32, 34-36, 56, 66-67, 84-85, 109, 112-113, 119, 125, 127, 130, 138, 152, 212-213, 229, 252, 259
customers 3, 17, 21, 30-32, 46, 66, 82, 96, 98, 102, 111, 116, 119, 130, 132, 155, 211, 215, 226, 252, 256
customize 73
customized 2, 35, 94, 98
cut-down 253
cycles 139
damage 3, 206
Dashboard 10, 104
dashboards 74, 87
database 54
databases 51, 53, 197
dataset 55, 242
day-to-day 84
deadlines 23, 98, 170
dealing 256
decide73, 77, 201, 270
decision 7, 66, 74, 136, 208, 232-233
decisions 60, 67, 78-79, 141, 220, 233, 237-239, 241, 247
dedicate 198
dedicated 9

deep-dive 41
deeper 12, 242
default 120
defect 40
defective 206
defects 49, 137, 228-229
define 4, 25, 149, 156, 200, 211, 232
defined 12, 17, 25, 27, 29, 31-32, 34-35, 37, 39, 49-50, 58, 65, 81, 92, 143, 147, 156, 159, 164, 182, 194, 201-203, 217, 220
defines 35, 176
defining 9, 139, 158
definite 81
definition 256
degree 182, 241-243, 249-250
-degree 2
delays 46, 166, 263
delegated 26, 255
delete 102
deletions 87
deliver 17, 21, 36, 75, 87, 112, 181, 186, 188, 240
delivered 22, 89, 125, 149, 176, 182, 221, 237, 243, 247, 261, 268
delivers 43
delivery 113, 122, 170, 173, 206, 222, 264, 267
Delphi 178
demand 115, 212, 255
demanded 110
demands 76, 242, 249
Deming 179
department 9, 119, 161, 226, 264
depend 226
dependence 113
dependent 149, 261
depict 172
deployed 35, 76, 82
deployment 47, 93, 97, 133
deposited 100
deputy 263
Describe 23, 78, 153, 179, 228, 257, 268
described 3, 230
describing 31
deserving 227

design 11, 20, 40, 50, 69, 74, 78, 83, 98, 105, 162, 211, 242, 247, 255
designated 148
designed 9, 11, 54, 56, 68, 76, 79, 243, 248
designing 9
desired 33, 191, 254
detail 156, 161-162, 164, 228
detailed 55-56, 136, 149, 157, 162, 166, 184, 247
detailing 256
details 222-223, 256
detect 83, 125
detective 59
determine 11, 59, 144, 166, 179, 189, 203, 219, 240
determined 26, 58, 196-197, 206, 213, 264
develop 65, 67, 159, 208, 242
developed 11, 25-26, 29-30, 44, 74, 76, 158, 166, 193, 196-197, 202, 216, 230, 244, 253-254
developer 68
developers 210
developing 53, 218
deviated 51
deviation 178, 245
device 234
devices 70, 72, 130
diagnose 212
diagram 5, 62, 145, 172, 183
diagrams 157, 203
dialogue 264
dictates 183
Dictionary 5, 161
differ 94, 178, 182
difference 42, 46, 54, 125, 176, 178, 187, 232
different 9, 27, 30, 32, 37, 44, 62, 92, 95, 104, 114, 128-129, 139, 143, 147, 164, 200, 269
difficult 33, 166
digital 108, 117
digitizing 57
diligence 52, 93
direct 198-199
direction 31, 145
directions 214
directly 3, 93, 141, 204, 269
directors 255

Directory 7, 237
Disagree 12, 17, 25, 39, 50, 65, 81, 92
disaster 61
disclosure 161
discount 103
discounts 89, 126
discovered 69
discovery 109, 122
discrete 229
display 47, 170
displayed 36, 44-45, 48, 57, 166
displaying 121
disposal 234
disputes 266
disregard 179
disrupt 63
divide 239
Divided 24, 26, 38, 49, 64, 79, 90, 134
document 11, 28, 136, 146, 152, 158, 193, 232, 237
documented 26, 44, 50, 69, 82, 84, 87, 89, 143, 156-158, 179, 200, 228, 259
documents 9, 178, 264
dollar 92, 251
dollars 162
Domains 94
double 265
downloaded 122
downtime 119
downward 110
dramatic 115
drawing 210
driving 77, 110
dropped 119, 252
duplicates 41
Duration 5, 144, 159, 178, 180
durations 31, 164, 182
during 31, 47, 75, 112, 137, 146, 169, 174, 192, 199, 202, 206, 210, 213, 264
duties 120
dynamic 106
dynamics 29
eagerly 2
earliest 149

earned 7, 253-254
easily 74, 78, 124
ecommerce 20, 121
economic 127, 214, 264
economical 147
ecosystem 93
ecosystems 31, 37, 92, 95, 97, 113
eDiscovery 232
edition 10
editorial 3
educate 113
educated 1
education 89, 255
effect 74, 210, 256, 269
effective 42, 60, 97, 164, 181, 234-235, 270
effects 170
efficiency 114, 235, 251
efficient 68, 73, 89, 101, 226, 271
effort 27, 162 163, 165, 246
efforts 34, 121, 261
either 105
electronic 3, 94, 107, 121, 129
element 198, 251
elements 11, 61, 116, 156, 161, 196, 229, 242, 251
eliciting 115
eliminate 214, 242
embarking 34
emblem 99
embrace 100
emerging 1, 85
employed 220
employee 40, 77, 125, 243, 257
employees 47, 60, 79, 83-84, 101, 104-105, 107, 114, 118-119, 123, 125-126, 131, 234, 243
employers 140, 235
employing 99
employment 221, 235, 256
empower 9, 99, 129
enable 112
enabled 129
encounter 78
encourage 79
encryption 28, 118

ending 110
Endpoint 102
energy 1
engage 241, 245
engagement 140, 204-205, 217
enhance 242
enlarged 210
enough 9, 154, 247, 261
ensure 28, 31, 75, 100, 114, 117, 138, 144, 150, 197, 237, 247
ensuring 11, 253-254
entail 53
Enterprise 97, 226
entire 182, 264
entities 42, 110, 235
entity 3, 151
entries 42
equally 122, 268
equation 70, 99
equipment 21, 112, 192
equipped 31
equitably 26, 239
equivalent 221
eQuotes 77
error-free 63, 116
errors 41, 109, 112, 137, 255-256
escalated 247
escalation 52, 63
essence 241
essential 84
establish 65, 189
estimate 46, 145, 178, 180, 182, 186, 219, 259
estimated 26, 30, 128, 189, 208-209, 257-258
estimates 5-6, 34, 62, 145, 157, 178, 182, 184, 186
estimating 5-6, 180, 184, 186, 188-189, 221
estimation 67, 147-148, 220
estimator 186
estimators 186
etcetera 46
ethical 65, 123, 193, 235, 259
evaluate 75, 202
evaluated 190, 219
evaluating 74, 264
evaluation 74-75, 218-219, 264

events 18, 179
Everyday 1
everyone 27, 37, 194
everything 232
evidence 12, 208-209, 226, 255-256, 263-264
evident 192
evolution 39
exactly 123
examined 263
Example 4, 10, 14, 158, 161, 242
examples 9-10
exceed 159
excellence 9
except 263
excess 198
excessive 104, 207
excited 1
exciting 243
exclude 50, 78, 127
execute 247, 259, 261
executed 39, 45, 230
Executing 7, 184, 224
execution 98, 108, 146, 192, 228
executive 9
executives 42
existence 162
existing 11, 84, 95, 108, 113, 121, 123, 131, 133, 138-139, 251
exists 172
expect 115, 145, 150, 180, 187, 269
expected 19, 31, 60, 102, 115, 132, 143, 145, 186, 225, 232, 252, 271
expecting 63
expense 198
expenses 21, 252
experience 28, 37, 106, 112, 115, 235, 257
expertise 73, 132, 145, 210, 256
experts 30, 179, 264
expiration 172
expire 62
expiring 107
explained 11
explicitly 99
explore 62, 116, 250

explored 192
exposure 208
extended 115
extensive 2
extent 12, 28, 144, 162
external 1-2, 34, 93, 194
facilitate 12, 51, 87, 94, 250
facilities 33, 210, 235
facility 99
facing 22
factor 218
factors 48, 144, 173, 188, 210
failed 46
failure 194, 214, 262
failures 47, 229
fairly 26
falling 26
fallout 111
familiar 10
fashion 3, 27
faster 105, 124
favorable 126, 251-252
favour 103
feasible 189, 208, 229
feature 11
features 112, 114, 129, 145, 206, 259
feedback 27, 30, 46, 106
feeling 1, 110
figure 40
filing 105
filings 119
filter 194-195
finalized 14
finance 98
financial 21, 57, 62, 70, 88, 133, 142, 206, 264-265
finding 108
findings 194
fingertips 11
finish 96, 138, 149, 166, 168, 172, 253-254
finished 138, 148, 170
fiscal 271
fixing 22
focused 42, 47, 203

focuses 137
folate 90
follow 87, 173, 240, 259
followed 36
following 10, 12, 193, 265
follow-on 261
follow-up 96
forecast 253
foresee 55, 170
foreseen 137
forget 11
formal 8, 157, 161, 203, 207, 220-221, 250, 259-260
formally 147, 184, 216
format 11, 94, 102, 114, 228, 238, 270
formats 123, 206
formed33, 35
formula 13
Formulate 25
formulated 147, 239
forward 2, 58
foster 209
frames 178
framework 83, 93, 196
fraudulent 59
frequency 37, 90, 196, 214
frequent 109, 148
frequently 43, 239, 250
friends 2
frustrated 113, 130
full-scale 74
fulltime 165
function 108, 141, 155-156, 165, 186, 260, 263, 268
functional 147
functions 44, 111, 124, 152, 176
funded190, 261
funding 107, 149, 157, 209, 249, 261, 264-265, 271
further 10, 49, 208
Fusion 87
future 9, 44, 46, 85, 88, 106, 162, 212, 244, 252
gained2, 63, 85, 90
gather 12, 39, 51
gathered 36, 41, 58
gathering 151, 221

gearing 42
general 96, 169, 234, 244, 247, 259
generally 226
generate 56, 63, 71, 109
generated 55, 63, 68, 94
generation 10
generic 2
geographic 18
geography 27
getting 2, 107, 185, 232
globally 95
Go-Live 105
governance 200
governing 204
government 270
graded 209, 228
granted 240
grants 255
graphical 182
graphs 10, 44
greater 127
ground 40, 57, 212
grouped 168
groups 141, 165, 199, 221, 227
growth 57, 115, 128
guaranteed 27
guarantees 72
guidance 106
guided 59
guideline 109
guidelines 100, 232, 263
guides 146
guiding 218
handle 106, 124, 174, 210, 237
handled 106, 117, 124, 161
handling 52, 234
happen 18, 61, 170, 214
happened 136, 146
happening 119
happens 9, 47, 63, 93, 102, 131, 152, 164, 189, 208-209, 214-215, 266
hardly 253
hardware 26, 37, 93, 108, 270

hashing 56
having 22, 264
hazards 214
hazmat 255
heading 97, 110
health 90, 124, 129, 206
heights 96
helpdesk 229
helped 69
helpful 46, 100, 199
helping 9, 118, 156, 224
hierarchy 95, 116
higher 129, 133
highest 43, 113, 130
high-level 29
highlight 2, 209
hiring 87
historical 74, 188
history 129, 167, 186
hitters 52
hitting 253
holiday 2
Honestly 2
hosted 115
hosting 117
hottest 128
humans 9
hypotheses 50
hypothesis 270
identified 3, 19, 25, 32, 44-46, 49, 54-55, 137, 155-156, 161, 165, 168, 192, 199-200, 208-209, 215, 220, 232, 237, 245, 268
identify 1, 11-12, 21, 23, 59, 65, 170, 178, 189, 202, 212, 229, 244, 245
illicit 126
images 151
imbedded 90
immediate 38, 40, 141, 236
impact 6, 28, 32, 40, 42-47, 49, 73, 85, 137, 151, 191, 207-212, 225, 228, 230, 238, 245, 248, 270
impacted 40, 44
impacting 48
impacts 46, 49, 141, 144, 180, 207, 220, 269
imperative 120

implement 23, 81, 119, 248
import 114, 120
importance 241
important 21, 55, 61, 93, 103, 114, 123, 141, 144, 176, 195, 205, 222, 241, 243
imported 48
importing 114
impression 101, 131
improve 4, 11, 40, 44, 55, 65, 68-69, 71-72, 75, 78, 136, 139, 158, 192, 194, 237, 243, 261, 269-270
improved 2, 69-71, 76, 89, 269
improving 43, 227
inaccurate 76, 113
inadequate 1
incentive 133
incentives 87, 121, 244
incident 208
include 68, 78, 128, 145, 147, 156, 167, 184, 198, 220, 242
included 4, 9, 66, 85, 117, 144, 152, 157, 188, 228, 257, 267
includes 11, 42
including 32-33, 37, 67, 118, 158, 164, 234, 245, 268
inclusion 234
in-coming 192
incomplete 76
incorrect 264
increase 42, 90, 157, 210, 251
increased 41-42, 52, 200
increasing 97
incumbent 103, 108
incumbents 103
Incurrence 198
indemnity 255
in-depth 10, 12
indicate 46, 86
indicated 83
indicators 19, 45, 115, 235
indirect 161, 187, 198, 251
indirectly 3
individual 43, 166, 239, 244, 257, 269
industries 72, 79
industry 1-2, 109-110, 120, 203, 235
ineligible 111
influence 93, 106, 140, 204-205, 232-233, 264

influences 205
inform 243
informal 249
informed 199, 241
ingrained 90
inhibit 70
in-house 2, 138, 193
initial 139, 192
initially 60, 150
initiated 188, 230
Initiating 4, 136
initiative 12, 196, 245
innate 113
Innovate 65
innovation 53, 57, 109, 264
innovative 181, 188
inputs 27, 31, 81, 147
inquiries 122
inquiry 110
insight 56, 127
insights 1-2, 10
inspection 208
instance 111, 124, 130
instead2, 87
insurance 124, 255-256
integrate 72, 87, 95
Integrated 60, 190
integrity 230
intend 66
intended 3, 66, 70
INTENT 17, 25, 39, 50, 65, 81, 92
intention 3
intentions 234
interact 47
interest 127, 130, 194-195, 214, 227
interested 268
interests 23, 205, 222, 264
interface 120, 123, 128
interfaces 25, 60
interfere 126
interim 243
internal 1, 3, 34, 119, 133, 142, 161, 194, 208, 255
interpret 12, 51, 70, 124

interrupt 103
interview 1
interviews 128
introduce 124
introduced 250
intuitive 111
invalid 102
inventory 61, 92
investing 2, 45
investment 28, 42, 193, 197, 207
invoice 238
invoices 185
invoicing 107
involve 104, 142
involved 17-18, 90, 136, 152, 155, 184, 199-200, 217, 221, 227, 246, 256, 267
involves 150
isolate 42
isolated 251
issues 52, 69, 136, 141, 148, 151, 155, 158, 174, 220, 245, 247, 252, 269, 271
iterative 151
itself 3, 22
joining 113
judgment 256
justify 208
keeping 43, 125
know-how 210
knowledge 1-2, 11, 28, 30, 34, 60, 63, 69-70, 85, 87-88, 90, 132, 179, 202, 222, 240, 267
labeled 199
language 76, 100
larger 88
latest 10
launch 133
leader 28, 54, 210
leaders 35, 38, 125, 164, 205, 242, 244
leadership 26, 109, 143
leading 111
learned 1, 8, 83, 197, 259, 268-270
learning 83, 88
legend 93
length 97, 240

lesson 268-269
lessons 8, 74, 83, 197, 259, 269-270
Leveling 168
levels 88, 127, 159, 199, 215, 256
leverage 32, 83, 188
leveraged 34
leveraging 53
lexical 126
liability 3, 255
licence 19
license 37
licensed 3
licensing 106
lifecycle 270
lifespan 271
Lifetime 11
Lightning 118
likelihood 70, 207-208
likely 89, 210, 212, 233
limited 11, 112, 120
limits 109
linear 44, 151
Linked 37, 233
listed 111, 196
little 2, 74
locally 66
located 18, 99, 107, 122
location 36, 99, 239
logical 172, 174
longer 1, 19, 63, 83
long-term 76, 82
looked 1
looking 84, 247
losing 112
losses 36, 44
lowest 173
magazine 263
maintain 81, 190
maintained 78, 118, 234, 249
majors 89
makers 66, 74, 109, 136
making 47, 53, 78, 104, 197, 208, 224

manage 30, 38, 40-41, 63, 76, 108, 138, 150, 153, 174, 182, 196, 202, 204, 212, 221, 246, 271
manageable 27, 74, 165
managed 9, 52, 77, 101, 112-113, 149, 228, 260
management 5-7, 10-11, 21, 32-33, 35, 47, 53, 57, 61, 66-69, 72, 77, 85, 106, 110, 133, 136, 141, 143, 145-147, 149, 155-156, 158, 161, 164-165, 177, 179-180, 183-184, 190, 192, 194, 196, 198, 202, 204, 206, 210, 213, 216, 219-220, 222, 224-226, 234-235, 240, 243, 247, 251, 253, 259, 266
manager 9, 11, 28-29, 74, 93, 138, 149, 178, 226, 259
managers 4, 65, 96, 135, 178-179, 199
manages 77, 146, 258
managing 4, 69, 127, 135, 140-141, 150, 179, 182, 235, 256, 269
mandatory 40, 230
manner 229, 242, 247, 259
manual 234, 263
mapped 28
mapping 63
margin 252
margins 131
market 18, 27, 73, 84, 86, 96, 103, 109, 113, 120, 122, 126, 132, 208, 218, 251, 253
marketable 208
marketer 9
marketing 55, 57, 95, 104, 121, 129-132
markets 21, 115, 117
markup 117
material 114, 161, 170, 192, 255
materials 3, 156, 234, 239, 270
matrices 153
Matrix 4-6, 141, 153, 198, 212
matter 30, 45, 242
matters 232
maximize 207, 243
maximizing 117
maximum 54, 98, 124
meaning 169
measurable 32, 35, 75, 162, 186, 249
measure 4, 11, 18, 31, 36, 39, 43-46, 65, 188-190, 194-195
measured 22, 81, 89, 162, 194, 214
measures 44-46, 86, 195, 242, 244
measuring 198

mechanical 3
mechanism 256
mechanisms 264
mediation 79
medium 242, 253
meeting 26, 34, 85, 136, 156, 185, 226, 232, 239-240
meetings 27, 29, 35, 136, 155, 199, 232, 240
member 7, 26, 99, 104, 176, 226, 239, 243, 245, 249
members 1, 27-28, 30, 32, 58, 75, 123, 165, 182, 184, 199, 204-205, 212, 217, 237, 239-243, 249-250, 270
membership 249, 263
mental 129
message 54
messages 204, 240, 269
method 106, 110, 116, 145, 169, 181, 192, 222, 241-242
methods 20, 30, 37, 158, 188, 211, 220, 240, 255
metric 52
metrics 6, 40, 87, 194-195, 202
middle 111
milestone 5, 170-171, 173
milestones 33, 140, 168, 172, 184
minimize 225, 248
minimum 98, 234, 256, 258, 264
minimums 98
minority 23
minutes 26, 185
missed 62
missing 63, 101
Mission 44, 215
Mitigate 225
mitigated 2, 206, 268
mitigating 77
mitigation 145-146, 210, 220
mixing 31
mobile 68, 70-72, 109
mobility 47, 97
mobilize 95
mobilized 144
Modeling 128, 197
models 18, 121, 157
modern 148, 256
modified 71, 128
moments 60

Monday 1
monitor 65, 85, 90, 148, 189
monitored 87, 137, 166, 178, 180
monitoring 7, 82, 84-87, 150, 174, 203, 206, 235, 247
monthly 98, 133
months 1, 33
morning 1
motivate 250
motivation 139
motive 197
movement 85, 179
moving 55-56
multiple 86, 104, 117, 123, 126, 220
naming 120
narrative 170
narrow 52
national 141, 144, 214, 224, 239, 265
nature 161
navigate 58
nearest 13
necessary 43, 57, 70, 100, 143, 148, 189-190, 199, 223, 237, 241, 270
needed 2, 19, 21, 23, 27, 63, 86, 89, 136, 147, 152, 180, 196, 198, 202-204, 222
negative 182
negatively 208
negatives 113
negotiable 119
neither 3
network 5, 40, 125, 172, 183, 249
networking 97
Neutral 12, 17, 25, 39, 50, 65, 81, 92
nights 122
nominal 263
non-cash 133
normal 90, 224
Notice 3
noticing 233
notified 223, 228, 267
number 24, 38, 49, 64, 79, 90, 124, 130, 134, 169, 199, 212, 272
numbers 97, 240
numerous 266

object 106, 114
objective 9, 141, 144, 162, 190, 217, 233
objectives 2, 21-22, 25, 37, 129, 133, 147, 151, 184, 190, 202-204, 208, 216, 220, 226, 249, 271
objects 83
observe 200
observed 71
obstacles 22, 181, 188
obtain 260, 269
obtained 27
obviously 12
occurred 192
occurrence 229
occurring 73, 137, 213
occurs 21, 137, 143, 194, 247
offered 49, 111-112
offering 86
offers 56, 104
off-hours 35
office 226, 267
Officer 1
officers 88, 255
officials 266
offline 59, 68
off-line 68
off-site 93
onboard 119
onboarding 217
on-call 35
one-time 9
one-to-one 129
ongoing 43-44, 81, 166, 180
on-going 148
online 37, 116
on-site 93, 237
opened 162
operate 190, 214
operating 7, 48, 83, 239-240
operation 85, 93, 112, 120, 181
operations 11, 87, 90, 122, 139
operators 50, 87, 264
opponent 233
optimal 66, 68, 73, 258

optimally 79
optimized 72, 77
optimiztic 178
option 97, 101, 255
options 21, 33, 49, 100, 107, 117, 123, 208
ordered 1
ordering 121, 264
orders 77, 116, 122, 263
organized 168
orient 85
oriented 202
original 148, 182, 233-234
originally 147, 164
originator 61
others 43, 127, 183, 188, 190, 192, 198, 204-205, 208, 211-212, 234, 255
otherwise 3, 70, 161, 243
outcome 12, 65, 141-142, 238, 271
outcomes 66, 71, 89, 96, 115, 181, 188, 254-256
output 31, 48, 56, 83, 86
outputs 31, 50, 81, 174
outreach 57
outside 24, 63, 79, 136, 241
Outsource 266
outsourced 224
outweigh 40, 42
overall 11-12, 22, 101, 131, 144, 151, 157-158, 223, 240, 257, 271
overcome 181, 188
overhead 161-162, 198-199, 251
overlook 245
oversight 147, 157, 193, 216, 243, 255
overtime 168
owners 159
ownership 42, 44, 88
package 161-162
packaged 19
packages 112, 162, 198
packaging 255
Padding 187
parallel 173
parameters 89, 148
Pareto 52, 203
particular 46, 84, 116, 122, 241, 247, 264

parties 2, 118, 148, 267
partner19, 111, 127
partners 17, 81, 90, 114, 142
passed39
pattern 169
payment 119, 124, 185, 264-266
payments 264-265
PC-based 124
pending 230
people9, 122, 126, 196, 198-199, 205, 210, 224, 227, 241, 247, 253, 261
percentage 153
perception 78
perform 27, 35, 82, 92, 115, 146, 176, 214, 259, 263
performed 93, 99, 153, 167, 206
performing 198, 208, 235
perhaps 254
period 79, 161
periodic 118, 184
periods229, 264
permission 3
permit 128-129
person 3, 41, 170, 186, 264
personal 72, 133, 270
personally 66, 153
personnel 87, 98, 102, 183, 196, 264, 270
pertinent 87
phases 168, 204, 247, 261, 269
philosophy 58, 111
phones 125
physical 78
placed125
placements 235
planned 39, 45, 81, 162, 164, 180, 220, 268-269
planning 4, 10, 83, 85-86, 90, 137, 143, 147, 155, 157, 162, 165, 174, 226, 234-236
platform 28, 72, 112
platforms 108
playing2
pocket188
pockets 188
pointing 117
points 24, 38, 49, 64, 79, 90, 134, 196-197

policies 234, 256
policy 58, 99, 116, 138, 174, 235, 263, 270
political 70, 170, 204, 210
politics 58
population 90
portfolio 127
portfolios 245
portion 2, 183
portray 52
position 61
positioned 188
positive 63, 145, 193, 204
positively 208
possible 46, 50, 52, 63, 68, 71, 76, 81, 241, 263
posted 42
potential 20, 73-75, 81, 117, 155, 209
practical 65, 74, 81, 226-227
practice 110, 116, 120, 147, 184
practices 11, 83, 87, 148, 184, 259, 263
practicing 129
praise 241
preaward 219
precaution 3
precede 172
predefined 33
predict 228
prediction 168
predictive 41, 59
predictor 199
predictors 125, 229
preferred 35, 222
pre-filled 10
premier 82
prepare 67, 196, 200, 204
prepared 1, 97, 133
preparing 183, 235, 269
prepay 132
presence 125
present 44, 88, 98, 222
presented 1, 238
presenting 234
preserve 29
pressure 110

pressures 170
prevent 44, 47, 157, 185
prevented 265
previous 34, 170, 257, 261
previously 146, 230
priced 109
prices 37, 102, 126, 252, 263-264
pricing 20, 35, 41, 50, 58, 60, 89, 102, 106-108, 113-114, 119, 121, 124, 126-127, 132
primarily 52, 203
primary 51, 139, 176, 178
principles 148, 218
priorities 47, 222
priority 43, 168, 241
private 144, 263
problem 17, 23, 25, 28, 32-34, 63, 151, 178, 227-228, 253
problems 17, 22-23, 42, 67, 73, 83, 143, 151-152, 155, 196, 219
procedure 132, 234, 256, 264
procedures 11, 69, 83-84, 87, 89, 158, 162, 174, 179, 182, 198, 220-221, 240, 265
proceed 270
process 4, 6-9, 11, 25, 27, 29, 31, 36-37, 40, 43-63, 65, 69, 71, 76, 83-90, 136, 138, 143, 146, 148-149, 151-153, 155-156, 158, 174, 179, 181, 190, 193, 196-197, 203, 207, 210, 212-213, 217-218, 224, 233, 237-238, 243, 247, 253-254, 256, 258-259, 261, 263, 269
processed 263
processes 1, 28, 44, 50, 53, 57-61, 87, 141, 143, 158, 162, 164, 197, 206, 225, 230, 234-235, 240, 244, 259, 264
processing 62
procure 86
produce 1, 143-144, 174, 225-226
produces 169
producing 153
product 3, 27, 40, 73, 101-102, 107-109, 111, 113, 127, 130-13[illegible], 139, 149, 156, 158, 178, 190, 194, 206-208, 212, 226-227, 237, 245, 253-254, 259, 261-262, 268, 270
production 104, 240
products 3, 22, 35, 37, 50, 62, 73, 86, 93, 96, 100, 107, 109, 11[illegible], 119-120, 126, 138, 143-144, 150, 154, 191, 211, 226
profile 33, 236
profiles 109
profit 42

program 21, 61, 79, 107, 120, 144, 187, 224, 244, 248
programs 144, 227, 245
progress 32, 144, 185, 189, 197, 224-225
project 4-5, 7-10, 20, 22-23, 29, 31, 47, 68, 86, 92, 99, 104-105, 115, 128, 130, 133, 135-151, 153, 155-159, 164-167, 170, 172-173, 176-186, 188-190, 192-193, 198, 200-204, 206, 208, 210-212, 216-217, 220-227, 230-231, 237-238, 245, 247-249, 253, 257, 259-261, 267-271
projected 190, 198-199
projects 4, 33, 46-47, 108, 135, 139, 142-144, 153, 178-179, 208, 221, 226-227, 245, 253-254, 261
promote 255
promoting 107
promotion 90, 200
promotions 124
promptly 247
prompts 106
proofing 71
proper 150
properly 38, 137, 161-162, 234
property 127, 133
proposal 170
proposals 218-219
proposed 23, 46, 66, 68, 145-146, 151, 257-258, 261
prospect 57
prospects 52, 82, 105
protecting 76
protocols 194
proved 259
provide 21, 69, 74-75, 77, 97, 102, 106, 116, 121, 123, 140, 150, 162, 172, 181, 188, 199, 224, 241, 247, 250-251, 255, 264
provided 2, 13, 26, 90, 148, 165, 178, 219, 223, 234, 270
provider 96
Providers 94, 103
provides 170
providing 86, 103, 107-108, 112, 140, 170
provision 232
public 102, 144, 217, 255, 263, 265
publicly 111
published 120
publisher 3
purchase 9, 77, 101, 104, 119, 218
purchasing 1-2, 263

purpose 4, 11, 116, 138, 156, 176-177, 189, 197, 232, 239, 242-243, 249-250
purposes 133, 162
pursuing 2, 110
purting 76
quadratic 99
qualified 27, 146
qualify 55
qualifying 183
quality 6-7, 11, 46, 51, 60, 72, 86, 112, 136, 141, 143, 155, 165, 179, 182, 184, 191-197, 201-203, 216, 234-235, 237, 247, 255-256, 264
question 12, 17, 25, 39, 50, 65, 81, 92
questions 9-10, 12, 178, 180, 204, 219, 236
quickly 11, 186
quotation 26, 53, 94, 99, 110
quotations 116, 122, 127, 130
quoted 112, 114
quotes 71, 76, 109, 113, 123
quoting 50, 101, 109, 116
racing 87
raised 155
rather 251
rating 228
ratings 218-219
rational 162
rationale 232, 251
reaching 222
readiness 148, 222
reading 100, 118
readings 90, 144
realistic 164, 182, 212, 242
reality 190
realize 2
realizing 1
really 9, 52, 107, 117, 198
reasonable 74, 147, 164, 256
reasonably 219
reasons 34, 119
rebrand 119
rebuttal 105
recast 186
receipts 100, 128

receivable 128
receive 10-11, 29, 77, 118, 133, 237
received 32, 116, 234, 242, 270
receiving 234
recent 94, 103
receptive 106
recipient 266
recognize 4, 17, 20-21, 241
recognized 20, 23, 245, 250
recommend 48, 155, 241
record 51, 124, 128, 240
recorded 112
recording 3
records 63, 67, 94, 106-107, 128-129, 199, 234, 267
recurring 26, 112
re-design 57
reduce 45, 49, 74, 113, 144, 157, 198, 242, 256
reduced 41
reducing 85
redundant 35, 104
references 272
reflect 63, 269
reflected 121
reforms 23, 46
refreshed 2
regard 26
regarding 23, 218, 227
Register 4, 6, 140, 208-209, 256
regular 32, 35, 63, 100, 257, 263
regularly 27-29, 60, 136
regulated 93
regulation 114, 116
regulators 61
regulatory 192, 211
relate 179, 225, 230
related 18, 86, 155, 204, 229, 245, 253, 269
relating 120, 255
relation 21, 264
relations 209
relative 39, 241
release 119, 204, 264, 269
released 229
releases 34, 69, 257

relevant 32, 83, 118, 185, 201, 223, 240, 252, 265
reliable 31, 52, 214, 234
relieved 2
relocate 57
relocation 145
remain 34, 131, 252
remaining 182, 189
remains 119
remedial 44
remedies 40
remember 103, 181
remotely 49
remove 53, 69, 214
removed 19
remunerate 77
repair 53
repeat 143
rephrased 11
replace 139
replaced 62
replanning 162
report 7, 42-43, 47, 70, 86, 90, 170, 185, 208, 218, 226, 234, 238, 249, 257, 269-270
reported 253
reporting 41, 57, 60, 74, 86, 116, 118, 149, 206, 221
reports 2, 59, 85, 94, 116, 133, 140, 148-149, 207, 228
repository 129
represent 51, 190-191, 261
reproduced 3
request 7, 68, 98, 133, 149, 190-191, 228, 230-231
requested 3, 78, 230
requests 98, 228
require 28, 31, 33, 35, 37-38, 174, 250
required 25-26, 28-31, 33-38, 54, 62, 142, 147, 149, 152, 166, 176, 186, 195, 197, 202, 204, 208, 213, 220, 234-235, 247, 263, 268
requiring 140, 266
research 18, 65, 69, 74, 171, 240
resemble 224
reserve 122
reserved 3
reserves 203
resistance 222

resolution 66, 72
resolve 237, 239
resolved 195, 247
resource 5-6, 69, 95, 104, 115, 117, 157, 174, 176-177, 202, 226, 234
resources 2, 4, 9, 23, 31, 33, 35, 37, 41-42, 49, 67, 79, 84, 88, 96, 104, 110, 112, 126, 131, 142, 144-145, 155, 165, 168-169, 176-177, 183, 188, 210, 220, 255
respect 3
respected 114
respective 143
respond 103, 126
responded 13
respondent 107, 131
responding 208
response 18, 21-22, 81-83, 86, 90, 105, 109, 115, 257
responses 66, 76, 218
responsive 180, 189
result 54, 65-67, 69, 74, 77, 79, 161, 186, 188, 190, 230, 250, 266, 268-269
resulted 73, 89
resulting 57, 77
results 10, 31, 36, 43, 65, 70-71, 75, 79, 89-90, 143-144, 162, 165, 168, 183, 186, 188, 192, 194, 197, 224-225, 256
Retain 92
retention 40, 69
retrieval 126
return 193, 197, 207
returns 212
Revenue 88
review 11, 55, 75, 145, 150, 172, 182, 194, 199, 208, 232, 240, 243
reviewed 25-26, 155, 216
reviewer 241
reviewers 242
reviews 155, 157, 162, 165, 172, 192, 207, 213, 244
revised 62, 89, 215
revisions 266
revisit 233
reward 43, 62, 227
rewards 87
rights 3, 114
risk-free 48
roadmap 55

robust 96
rolled 95
roll-out 222
rounded 132
routine 88
routinely 199
routing 45, 94, 97
running 76, 90, 94
safety 74, 145
Salesforce 3-15, 17-24, 26-38, 41-43, 45, 47-50, 52, 57, 62-64, 66, 68-70, 73, 76, 78, 80, 82-84, 86-89, 91, 93-94, 100, 109, 111-112, 114, 120-122, 124, 134-151, 153, 155-159, 161, 164-168, 170, 172-174, 176-186, 188-190, 192-194, 196, 198-204, 206, 208, 210-212, 214, 216-218, 220-228, 230, 232, 234, 237-239, 241, 243, 245, 247-249, 251, 253-255, 257, 259-261, 263, 266-271
sample 178, 192
sampling 203
satisfied 41, 72, 150, 259, 262
satisfies 253
savings 34, 62, 69
scarce 42
scenario 36
scenes 2
schedule 5, 29, 46, 67, 89, 104, 120, 145, 162, 164-165, 172-173, 182-184, 191, 208-209, 216, 221, 230, 257, 268
scheduled 136, 149
schedules 103, 119, 182-183, 208
scheduling 162, 184
scheme 58, 82, 105, 118
Science 59, 181
scientific 181
Scorecard 4, 13-15
scorecards 87
Scores 15
scoring 11
Screen 228
screens 118
scripts 158
search 117, 128-129
searches 51, 54
seasons 61
second 13
secret 2, 56

secrets 1
section 13, 24, 38, 49, 64, 79-80, 90-91, 134
sections 193
sector 253
secured 255
security 73, 140, 230
seeing 23
seemingly 264
segment 218
segmented 32
segments 30, 252
select 125
selected 35, 66, 78, 147, 188-189, 223, 244
selecting 67
selection 6, 128, 218-219, 241
self-help 2
sellers 3
selling 47, 59, 103, 107
-selling 252
senior 110, 242
sensitive 133
sentiment 94, 96
separated 163
sequence 172
sequencing 144
series 12
serious 115
server 115
Service 1-4, 9, 26, 62, 78, 102, 104, 109, 113, 116, 132, 190, 208, 226-227, 271
services 3, 26, 29, 35, 40, 49, 60, 73, 86, 92, 100-101, 103-104, 108, 112, 130, 209, 224, 234, 240, 247, 252, 257-258, 260, 266
session 166
setting 103
several 264
severely 57
severity 209
shared 85, 188
sharing 63, 69, 136, 251
shield 28
shifted 211
shifts 71
shopping 1

shortening 95
short-term 207, 242
should 9, 18, 23, 29, 37, 42, 52, 59-60, 62, 69, 71-72, 76, 86, 95-96, 98-101, 111-112, 116, 119-120, 123, 128-130, 132, 140, 146, 149, 156, 158, 166-168, 170, 176-177, 180, 186, 196, 200, 207, 218-219, 224-225, 228-229, 237-238, 244, 247-248, 251, 263, 269
-should 190
showing 143
signal 132
signatures 174
signers 266
similar 29, 34, 52, 99, 167-168
simple 249, 253
Simply 10
single 51, 59, 93, 123, 130, 251
single-use 9
situation 2, 18, 39, 144, 183, 208, 210, 217, 253
situations 82, 127
skills 21, 43, 137, 148, 179, 186, 202-203, 224, 241-242, 249-250, 261, 270
slippage 210
slowing 55
smaller 50
smoothly 101
soccer 1
social 78, 96, 121, 214
socialize 95
software 21, 26, 31, 34, 37, 84, 94, 97, 106, 116, 123, 130, 143, 157-158, 212, 219, 223, 229, 257, 270
solely 35
solicit 30
solution 1, 39, 44-45, 57, 59, 62, 65-79, 81, 85, 155, 157, 257-258
solutions 68, 70-71, 74-75, 78-79, 85, 209
Someone 9
something 156-157, 190
sometimes 67
sophomore 125
sought 127
source 6, 19, 75, 106-107, 124, 129, 214, 218-219, 234
sources 52, 56, 62, 69, 108, 117, 128, 212
special 30, 90, 138, 219, 222
Specialist 101

specific 10, 22, 27, 32, 35, 103, 106, 113, 133, 149, 158, 166, 170, 174, 200, 203, 217, 220, 227, 230, 269
specified 124, 214, 261, 268
specifies 131
spelling 96
spending 2, 89
sponsor 21, 138, 148, 156, 179, 259
sponsored 28
sponsors 17, 136, 222, 242, 255
stability 48
stacks 129
staffed 33
staffing 87, 157, 165
staffs 98
stages 263
standard 9, 83-85, 147, 174, 178, 184, 194, 251, 257
standards 11-12, 82, 90, 158, 161, 193-194, 230, 263
started 10, 170, 173
starting 11
startup 138
stated 107, 162, 240, 264
statement 5, 12, 67, 148, 155-156, 158, 161, 186, 217, 236
statements 13, 24, 32-33, 38, 49, 63-64, 79, 91, 134
static 228
statistics 155
Status 7, 18, 21, 90, 148, 150, 226, 238, 253, 257, 270
statute 211
steering 147, 157, 193, 216
storage 96, 102, 228
stored 39, 51
strategic 147, 184, 220, 255-256
strategies 75, 157, 220, 223, 232-233
strategy 22, 26, 43, 55, 90, 97, 100, 107, 119, 123, 131, 133, 204, 251, 264, 269, 271
stratify 194
stream 128
strengths 239, 259
strong 179, 201, 255
Strongly 12, 17, 25, 39, 50, 65, 81, 92, 229
structure 5, 54-55, 67-68, 100, 113, 131, 159, 176, 223
structured 108, 165, 218
structures 126, 250
struggle 41

subdivided 162
subject 10-11, 30
subjects 78, 133
submission 26
submit 124
submitted 230-231
subsystems 79
sub-teams 241
succeed 125, 129, 250
success 18, 20, 30, 36, 44, 54, 82, 144, 173, 203, 216, 226, 232, 248
successful 1, 65, 69, 74-75, 85, 104, 136, 176, 227, 268
suddenly 210-211
suffered 242
sufficient 144, 247, 263-264
suggest 101, 228, 236
suggested 83, 190-191
suitable 20-21, 44, 56
summarize 51
summarized 161
Sunday 1
superior 1
supervisor 201, 243
supplied 101
supplier 77, 132
suppliers 20, 31, 50, 106, 111-112, 216, 263-264
supplies 259
support 3, 9, 23, 35, 45, 66, 68, 70-71, 85, 90, 96, 101, 105-107, 111, 114, 116, 122-123, 130, 141, 148, 174, 222, 233-234, 257
supported 33, 60, 100, 103, 123, 130, 224
supporting 196, 220, 264
supportive 148
surface 83
surrounded 132
suspended 131
SUSTAIN 4, 92
sustaining 82, 142, 239
symbols 120
symptom 17
system 11, 43, 54, 56, 58, 65, 75, 78, 84-85, 93, 97, 101-102, 104, 106, 108, 111, 118, 121, 124, 129, 151-152, 162, 198-199, 229-230, 233-235, 247, 251, 253-254

systems 1, 20, 42, 53, 55, 61-62, 70, 87, 97, 103, 105, 141, 155, 161, 220-221, 234-235, 251, 253
tables 157
tablet 72
tactics 233
Taguchi 179
tailored 2
takers 155
taking 76, 85, 136, 226
talent 131
talents 203
talking 9
tangible 256
target 32, 107-108, 244
targets 186, 253
tasked 88
teaming 239-240
technical 31, 70, 109, 112, 132, 143, 145, 170, 179, 207, 218-219
technique 178
techniques 136, 147, 185
technology 1, 20, 40, 77, 110, 127, 138, 152, 179, 208, 239-240
template 124
templates 9-10
tenant 56
tender 264
tested 68
testing 66, 74, 151, 193, 255-256
themselves 1
therein 162
things 136-137, 186, 194, 206, 212, 224, 247, 262
thinking 59, 79, 107, 118
thorough 228
thoroughly 96
thought 205
threat 242
threats 1-2, 185
through 51, 58, 93-94, 107, 123, 161, 242, 256
throughout 3, 172, 252
Thursday 1
tickets 121
time-bound 32
timeframe 189

timeline 98, 133, 158, 230, 248
timely 27, 118, 161, 229, 239, 247, 270
Timescales 170
timing 212
todays 179
together 240, 243
tolerable 148, 215
tolerance 97
tolerances 245
tolerated 166
toolkit 1-2
toolkits 1-2
top-down 83
topics 202
toward 85, 226
towards 2, 110, 121, 144
traceable 162
traced 157
tracked 92, 184
tracking 21, 27, 101, 150, 157
traded 111
trademark 3, 120
trademarks 3, 120
trading 112
trained 30, 33, 38, 105, 157, 212
training 23, 87, 89-90, 202, 222-224, 227, 240, 243, 255
Transfer 13, 24, 38, 49, 64, 80, 87-88, 91, 134, 222, 258
transition 150
translate 21
translated 35
transport 255
travel 198
treasurer 263
trending 192
trends 109, 145, 155, 214
triggered 164
triggers 110, 217
troubling 98
trunking 123
trusted 77
trying 9, 84, 194
typical 106, 110, 224
typically 59

unable 95, 240, 263
unaware 1
unclear 30
uncovered 2
underlying 51, 69
understand 36, 61, 70-71, 84, 136, 149, 178, 183, 200, 212, 241
understood 70, 74, 250
undertake 58, 206
underway 78
unhappy 111
unified 94
unique 2
uniquely 245
Unless 9
unlimited 124
unopened 162
unprepared 1
unresolved 174
update 1, 54, 63, 96, 106, 124, 182, 190
updated 10-11, 62-63, 184, 203
updates 11, 87, 106, 118, 257
updating 63, 203
upfront 222
upgrade 34, 58
upgrades 106
up-keeping 21
usability 74
usable 161
useful 75, 86, 157, 159, 207-208, 270
usefully 11
UserID 170
usually 1
utility 180
utilized 37, 79, 97
utilizing 1, 73, 129
validate 45, 254
validated 25, 29, 55
Validation 254
validity 247
valuable 9, 117, 121
values 110, 161-162, 214
variable 51
variables 48, 62, 83, 232

variance 7, 162, 241-242, 251-252
-variance 187
variances 161, 178, 184, 198, 251
variants 264
variation 17, 31, 44-45, 47-48, 52, 62, 85
variations 152
variety 70
various 83
vendor 35, 77, 107-108, 115, 129, 131, 164, 172, 185
vendors 63, 94, 110, 120, 123, 185, 202, 216
verified 11, 25, 29, 55, 171
verify 41, 43, 45, 48, 88, 182, 190, 253, 267
verifying 48
version 34, 94, 100, 104, 116, 257, 272
versioning 129
versions 27, 37
versus 112, 132
vertical 129
vested 214
viable 85, 159
viewed 122
viewpoint 269
viewpoints 269
violate 271
violation 123
violations 157
virtual 113
viruses 22
vision 26, 99, 145
visitors 105
visual 18, 46, 113, 195
visualize 166
vocabulary 99
voices 140
voided 265
volume 251
voluntary 42
vulnerable 141
waited 2
walking 2
warning 164
warrant 237
warranty 3, 53, 84, 228

wasted117
weaknesses 126, 158, 170, 219, 259
website 229
weekly 136
weeknights 1
whether 9, 102, 201, 263, 268, 270
-which 212
Whitelist 94
willing 191, 213
windfall 148
winning 110, 263
win-win 123, 131, 133
wisely 63
within 1-2, 18, 26, 58, 72, 79, 162, 166, 169, 180, 194, 214, 223, 227, 230, 234, 260
without1, 3, 13, 47, 126, 151, 230, 255, 266
workdays 209
worked 78, 121, 158, 216
workers 99
workflow 61-62, 233
workflows 77
workforce 55, 71
working 2, 33, 66, 143, 158, 232, 270
work-life 201
Worksheet 5-6, 180, 188
worried 242
worst-case 36
writing 75, 150, 153, 192
written 3, 76, 148, 234-235, 263
yearly 21
youhave 166
yourself 200

Made in the USA
Columbia, SC
20 September 2021

45837048R00193